Change Maker

"Well-written and insightful, this book would be extremely helpful for anyone wondering if after-death communication is possible, and if grief can be inspiring as well as heartbreaking."
—TERRI DANIEL, Founder of the Afterlife Conference

"*Change Maker*, although a story about a brother's death, is more an inspirational book of hope. On every page, author Rebecca Austill-Clausen courageously wields that hope as a machete to cut through her grief and, with the adroit use of visual imagery and humor, imbues the reader with a sense of comfort that we never really 'lose' those we love. That said, as she has with her brother, David, we can and must continue to keep our relationships with them alive. After all, love knows no boundaries, even death."
—ELISA MEDHUS, MD, author of *My Son and the Afterlife: Conversations from the Other Side* and *My Life After Death: A Memoir from Heaven* and creator of *ChannelingErik.com*

"With care and compassion, Rebecca Austill-Clausen shares her journey of letting go of ordinary reality and experiencing a deeper connection with her loved one. Her earnest struggles to open her mind and acknowledge new possibilities, may just help you discover your own willingness, awakened possibilities, and healing."
—TAMA KIEVES, best selling author of *A Year without Fear: 365 Days of Magnificence* and *Inspired & Unstoppable: Wildly Succeeding in Your Life's Work*

"A beautifully written personal story of a shared human experience—a loss of a beloved other and the life that unfolds thereafter. Rebecca's path, following her brother's death, leads her into the non-ordinary realms of the Mystery associated with the known tangible world, familiar to those who practice shamanism and walk in the dreamtime. She generously shares her gained wisdom and growth, as well as her poignant suggestions and support so others can explore the possibilities for themselves. How blessed are we, who with the help of someone who has gone before us, can begin to perceive the true magic that surrounds us and experience first hand the awakening and empowerment that always awaits us? Very blessed, indeed!"

—JILL KUYKENDALL, Physical Therapist and co-author with Hank Wesselman of *Spirit Medicine: Healing in the Sacred Realms*

"The writing is beautiful, precise and so very personable. *Change Maker* is one of those books that captures you from the first page! Becky's approach to spirituality is practical, yet invites your own spirit to soar. Reading it lifts you into new possibilities to see your own process of awakening as unique and wonderful as you are."

—JONETTE CROWLEY, author of *The Eagle and the Condor: A True Story of an Unexpected Mystical Journey*

"The passing of a loved one can have a profound spiritual transformation for family and friends. Rebecca Austill-Clausen tells us her journey of transformation from living a life of a stressed out workaholic businesswoman to becoming someone who is connected to her inner self. With Nancy Arael as a shamanic guide, Rebecca gives us a first hand view of the multitude of dimensions available to guide us and help us live in a more connected and rewarding way. This is a must read for anyone who has lost a loved one or is starting their own spiritual journey."

—DAVID BENNETT, author of *Voyage of Purpose: Spiritual Wisdom from Near-Death Back to Life* and *A Voice as Old as Time: Contemplations for Spiritual Transformation*

"Becky shares a descriptive and intimate personal example of a spiritual path unfolding and coming into existence. She portrays the delicate challenge between living in different worlds of reality and truth and reason. Becky paints a complex image of her spiritual journey by sharing her professional conflicts and doubts and how she eventually opened up and embraced that journey. Becky writes with openness, clarity, humor and great compassion and heart. This book is a jewel to read. It will cause pause for consideration and provide delight allowing wondrous possibilities of another life to emerge."
—TAMERA HUMBERT, D.Ed, OTR/L editor of *Occupational Therapy and Spirituality: A Conceptual Model for Practice and Research.*

"If you are a person who doubts life, believes that what you see in your everyday reality is all there is, or if you want to enter a timely doorway through which you can access a greater and more holistic view of life—then Rebecca Austill-Clausen's book is for you. Instead of her brother's death being an ending that she dreaded, it became a beginning that she was able to embrace. Just as many have before her, the author learns that while death is an illusion, life is continuous. Physical form and expression may change, but consciousness continues."
—MICHAEL J. ROADS, author *Through the Eyes of Love trilogy, Stepping … Between … Realities and Insights of a Modern Mystic*

"*Change Maker* is a courageous and compelling account of the author's spiritual discovery and triumphant evolution. An instant classic that will inspire and empower countless others to embark upon their own illuminating journey."
—WILLIAM STILLMAN, award-winning author of *The Soul of Autism: Looking Beyond Labels to Unveil Spiritual Secrets of the Heart Savants* and *Autism and the God Connection*

"*Change Maker* takes us on a journey into the healing power of shapeshifting. Rebecca's experiences remind us that we, and all sentient life, are one with a universal webwork of love and energy—in this worldly life as we know it, and beyond."

—LLYN ROBERTS, MA, award-winning author of *Shapeshifting into Higher Consciousness: Heal and Transform Yourself and Our World with Ancient Shamanic and Modern Methods*, co-author of *Shamanic Reiki: Expanded Ways of Working with Universal Life Force Energy*, and co-author of *Speaking with Nature: Awakening to the Deep Wisdom of the Earth*

"In her new book *Change Maker*, Austill-Clausen shows us how a powerful and painful experience, such as her beloved brother's illness and death, is often a catalyst for deep spiritual transformation."

—TANIS HELLIWELL, author of *Summer with the Leprechauns: A True Story* and *Pilgrimage with the Leprechauns: A True Story of a Mystical Tour of Ireland*

"*Change Maker* brings the fortunate reader along on an adventure of the heart as Becky Austill-Clausen recounts the journey that began with the death of her brother, David. Her story brims with discovery and all the understandable doubts that accompany big changes. Most striking is the author's deep curiosity about the spiritual realm that opens to her in David's hospital room. Her journey takes her to a new consciousness where opposites unite, where life and death, body and soul, energy and matter reveal themselves as a singular wholeness."

—EMMA MELLON, PhD, author of *Waking Your Dreams: Unlock the Wisdom of Your Unconscious* and *Still Life: A Parent's Memoir of Life Beyond Stillbirth and Miscarriage*

"A deeply personal and moving account of one woman's spiritual journey and realization of the true power of love in our lives. Austill-Clausen's story and suggested meditations and exercises will help anyone looking to connect more completely with their soul and life purpose."

—JENNIFER B. MONAHAN, author of *This Trip Will Change Your Life: A Shaman's Story of Spirit Evolution*

"This is a beautifully and delicately written book about the heart and soul's plight through grief and loss and culminates in a series of experiences that opens our author into worlds not ordinarily known. This work follows an ancient path whereby the boundaries of inner and outer worlds collapse. The initiate is led through the mists of time, guides and healing agencies arrive and revelations of deep mystery and nature are shared. The neophyte is initiated into the deeper mysteries of life and death and in turn is herself reborn."
—SUSAN MCCLELLAN, Shamanic Teacher

"From her unexpected awakening…to her discovery that energy can be seen and felt…to her realization that consciousness has no limits, Austill-Clausen deftly weaves a story of unfolding that has clarity, simplicity, and power. This book should be read by anyone experiencing the awakening of consciousness."
—PENNY KELLY, author of *The Elves of Lily Hill Farm: A Partnership with Nature*

Change Maker

Published 2016
Printed in the United States of America
ISBN: 978-1-63152-130-0 pbk
ISBN: 978-1-63152-129-4 ebk
Library of Congress Control Number: 2016939349

Second printing, 2019

For information, address:
She Writes Press
1563 Solano Ave #546
Berkeley, CA 94707

Cover and interior design by Tabitha Lahr
Illustrations by Micki McAllister
Images on pages i, vii, ix, xi, xiii, xiv, and xv © 123rf.com

She Writes Press is a division of SparkPoint Studio, LLC.

Dedicated to my awesome brother,
David Elliott Austill.
Thank you for opening my heart to adventures
previously unimagined.
I love you David,
always and forever.

Change Maker

How My Brother's Death
Woke Up My Life

Rebecca Austill-Clausen

SHE WRITES PRESS

The World I Live In

I have refused to live
locked in the orderly house of
reasons and proofs.
The world I live in and believe in
is wider than that. And anyway,
what's wrong with *Maybe?*

You wouldn't believe what once or
twice I have seen. I'll just
tell you this:
only if there are angels in your head will you
ever, possibly, see one.

—MARY OLIVER
Pulitzer Prize Winner

Contents

Chapters

✳ *Chapter 1* ✳

Transformation (OCTOBER)

The shell must break before the bird can fly.
—ALFRED TENNYSON

A massive animal stares into my soul. I am submerged in deep ocean waters, mesmerized, unable to move. The sea creature hovers before me, its deep brown eyes a match for my own.

The water shimmers with the promise of the rising sun, and slowly, cautiously, the marine mammal eases toward me, never breaking eye contact.

This creature is ancient, weathered, wrinkled. Its gigantic, rotund body connects directly to its head without the benefit of a neck. Its broad pug nose looks squished on its wizened face. Although the animal has no back crest or dorsal fin, its bifurcated tail reminds me of a very fat dolphin's.

Enthralled, I lose all concept of time.

As the creature hovers closer, I am suddenly engulfed in love—a feeling so broad, so wide, so all-encompassing that it defies description. I am beyond captivated, beyond awestruck. I am bathed in love.

In an instant, the creature's spirit enters my heart: I feel a jolt of emotional intensity, followed by a rush of fireworks bursting into ecstasy. My soul expands exponentially. Clarity bubbles up through me, and I feel a lightness, a deep knowing about life and afterlife that I have never experienced before. A profound flash of insight shocks me into understanding:

This animal holds the essence of my brother, David.

David, who lies in the hospital bed where he will spend his final hours as the machines keeping him alive dutifully pump air into his lungs. The hospital room where his friends and family have been saying good-bye, and where I have been keeping watch tonight.

David's spirit unites with mine in an intoxicating song of awareness. Secrets of the universe stream through me—some new, some old, all affirmed: We are one. There is no death, only life; we do not die but pass into a different realm of existence. Our souls retain our life force forever. We do not cease to exist when our earthly life ends; we just change shape. Our spirit, the core of special energy that makes each of us unique, will continue to thrive even as our bodies falter and wither away.

For the first time in my life, I glimpse eternity. Truth resonates inside me, a thrum of joy permeating every cell of my body.

I feel David's energy slowly leave, and my attention gradually turns outward. This animal that holds David's energy is swimming away, clearly comfortable in the ocean.

A new movement catches my eye. A small version of the same fat, dolphinlike creature has joined David. My heart vibrates with delight as I realize that this newcomer holds Edward's essence.

Edward and David have been best friends since elementary school, and I've always enjoyed seeing Edward. He recently passed from Earth, and I was not there to say good-bye. I send love to Edward, thrilled to be with him again and relieved that he will accompany David on the next stage of life's journey.

David, or the animal that holds his spirit, turns and gazes at me again. His eyes reflect eons of shared memories. Our souls meld as we acknowledge eternal life.

David turns away. He looks confidently at Edward and, with a jaunty flip of their tails, they swim off together through the clear blue waters.

I feel content for the first time in months.

My brother David is alive!

I open my eyes slowly and take a deep breath. I review this life-experience. My excitement grows. My heart pounds. I explode with the enormity of it. Somehow I just communed with David's life force from a different realm of existence. A gigantic grin stretches across my face, and I laugh out loud.

I know, with the confidence that arrives when something feels absolutely right, that David's spirit lives. I have never felt anything so powerful, so encompassing, and so real.

✳ ✳ ✳

Seven days earlier, I was an ordinary business owner sitting in my office on an ordinary business day. My assistant rushed into my office to tell me that my parents were on the phone. My parents never call me at work.

It was 10:11 A.M. on a Thursday.

Dad spoke calmly but urgently. "David's been rushed to the hospital in an ambulance. We're leaving now to meet him at Beth Israel Deaconess. Pam and Jiffy are already on their way."

Tears cascaded down my face. David always said if he left

3

home in an ambulance, he would never return. He was only thirty-seven.

"What happened?" I said, jotting down a note to my waiting assistant that asked her to please check flight schedules now.

Mom replied, factual and no-nonsense. "Loreen found him stumbling around his bedroom, unable to give himself his daily shots. When she asked if he needed help, he couldn't respond. After a few moments, he agreed to let her call an ambulance, but he refused to lie on the 'stretcher of death' and walked down two flights of stairs and into the ambulance under his own power."

My voice cracked as I promised to catch the first flight out, which should put me in Boston by early afternoon.

I hung up the phone, my tears flowing freely. My assistant handed me flight options from Philadelphia to Boston, and we chose one that gave me barely enough time to rush home, pack, and drive the hour to the airport. I called my husband as I left the office.

Jeff had been waiting for this call, too. He was calm, offering the reassurance I needed. "I'll take care of Ken and Ryan. Should we get them out of preschool and fly out tonight?"

My mind whirled as I tried to gauge the seriousness of the situation. David had been sick for seven years and getting progressively worse. Was this a false alarm?

I had not thought about Jeff and the kids coming to be with David also.

"Let me get there first. I'll call you."

"OK, Becky. Don't worry about the kids. Love you."

I threw basic necessities into my suitcase, paused for a minute, then tossed in my black suit, hoping I wouldn't need it. I raced to the airport, calling my assistant en route to clarify work details to be reorganized, meetings to be rescheduled, fending off the chaos I hoped wouldn't erupt during my absence.

With minutes to spare, I slid into my seat as the plane doors closed.

During the bumpy ride to Boston, I reviewed work priorities and finally thought about Jeff and the kids. Jeff is a great parent. I'd started my business eleven years earlier, and hundred-hour work weeks were common. Jeff's quiet, loving manner and offbeat humor supported us all. Our family was thriving, and we all loved Uncle David. I knew they would be OK without me at home.

A couple of hours later, I stood in the doorway of David's private hospital room, trying to catch my breath. He was lying on his back, the bed almost flat. The starched white sheets drawn up to his chin emphasized his incredibly skinny torso. His face was so pale that his eyes, always large, loomed enormous; they dominated his face. He struggled to smile and said, "Hi, Becky. Sorry you had to leave work to come see me."

Tears glistened in my eyes and threatened to overflow as I bent down to give David a kiss. *Family always comes first,* I told my staff, but personally I never seemed to follow this philosophy. Disappointed with myself, I slowly shook my head and said, "David, I'm so sorry."

He closed his weary eyes and seemed to drift off to sleep.

I looked around the room. My parents, my two sisters, and Loreen, David's best friend and roommate, were all there. We shared small, sad greetings but soon left the room, one at a time, as David slept. I was the last one out.

Over the next several days, we all saw David slipping away rapidly, despite the excellent care the nurses gave him. Each night I called Jeff, and each night my news was progressively worse.

David's doctor knew him well. He warned us that David had only a few days left to live.

I felt like a leaf adrift on a stormy sea, barely able to keep afloat, surrounded by gargantuan waves of sorrow and confusion. During the day, when David was asleep and I couldn't stand to wait anymore, I wandered the hospital halls aimlessly and found no comfort. I kept passing a sign that said "Meditation Room" and finally decided to open the door.

Sunlight streamed softly through a multi-hued stained-glass window. The colored light infused the room with a peaceful glow.

I sank into a chair at the back and closed my eyes. I breathed deeply and tried to calm my unsteady emotions.

I thought about Edward, who had passed away just six months ago. I implored Edward to take care of David.

Edward's smiling face appeared! His body began to grow and grow and grow until his head touched the ceiling. He looked about twelve feet tall.

He was a large fellow, 6' 7" by the time he was full-grown. I remember him bending his whole body to fit through our kitchen door.

Now he filled the room. Flowing, shoulder-length blond hair framed his friendly face. His huge grin radiated acceptance and peace.

I accepted Edward's presence without question. His familiar spirit calmed me, and I grasped his lifeline of support and held on without question. I soaked up his love like a dry sponge cupped in a warm and gentle bath.

Edward slowly stretched out his arms to form a cross with his body.

I heard his voice clearly in my mind. "I will help David," he said. "He will be well cared for."

I was enormously relieved. "Thank you, Edward. Thank you so much."

I breathed deeply. My eyes remained closed. I felt peaceful for the first time since the phone call from Mom and Dad that had brought me there.

I had no doubt that David was going to be all right. Edward would be with him.

My vision of Edward slowly faded.

I didn't know it then, but that was my first meditative experience with a loved one from another realm. It would not be my last.

* * *

The next few days passed in a blur. Throughout, I remembered Edward's message and experienced an inner calmness I'd never felt before.

David smiled in quiet acknowledgement as dozens of his friends came to visit one last time. I gave each of them heartfelt hugs of love and support. David flitted in and out of consciousness. He never complained.

Granny and Auntie Belle's visit was the most heart-wrenching. It seemed incomprehensible that these ancient matriarchs, pillars of our family and still healthy and vital at ninety and ninety-two, must say goodbye to their grandson and grand-nephew, who would not live to see his thirty-eighth birthday.

Granny raised herself out of her wheelchair, leaned over David, and gave him a kiss. Auntie Belle hobbled to David's side, balancing without help on her recently replaced knees. Granny stroked David's brow, murmuring quietly. He smiled.

I remembered visits with them—always an adventure, often involving treasure hunts on Cape Cod, always organized by Granny and Auntie Belle. I remembered stories of their adventures, and how those stories became part of who we were now.

Long before my dad and his only brother, Allen, were born, Granny and Auntie Belle were avid hikers. Their Longs Peak mountaineering adventures in the 1920s were legendary, memorialized in books and showcased at the YMCA of the Rockies in Estes Park, Colorado.[1-2]

Both women were missionaries who travelled the world ministering to those less fortunate. They spent years in Japan and India. The Thanksgiving holiday was always at Granny and Gramps' seaside home by the Atlantic, and two or three international guests always joined us at the table.

I remembered the annual day-after-Thanksgiving treasure hunt. All the grandkids and some parents cavorted around seaweed-covered boulders, peered under ancient stone bridges, hunted for clues hidden in the wildflower garden. We ran for hours, untangling fun jigsaw messages. Mohamed, our adopted cousin from Morocco, was the best puzzle solver. But David and our cousin Chris surged ahead after interpreting the last clue, ready to claim the prize: packages of Fiddle Faddle caramel corn and nuts nestled in Granny's furoshiki, a Japanese silk cloth that she wrapped up in mysterious ways. We gobbled down the treats, laughing raucously, proclaiming victory.

* * *

By the next morning, David was in a coma and not expected to live through the night. The doctor said he could pass at any moment; we were all just waiting. I could not bear the thought of David's dying alone, so I asked if I might spend the night in his room. Mom, Dad, and the nurses agreed.

I tossed and turned on the narrow, well-used portable twin mattress placed beside David's bed. A thin white sheet covered the soft plastic. It crunched each time my cramped body shifted, but I finally dropped into a restless sleep.

At 3 A.M., I bolted awake. I was so cold that I was shivering. I glanced over at David's body.

I watched his chest quickly rise, pause, and fall, timed

exactly with the ventilator's noisy *whoosh*. Up, down, as constant as a metronome, one mechanical breath after the other.

I felt no emotion, no essence, and no energy from David. Somehow I knew his soul had left his body. His body was empty, bereft of life. Yet his physical frame still breathed. Nighttime beepers from the hospital corridor made their demands. Time marched on, beating with an exact rhythm of nothing.

I rubbed my arms and trembled.

"What should I do?" I said out loud. What are you supposed to do when you are alone with your beloved brother's still-breathing dead body?

David's essence was gone. There was no reason for me to stay.

I considered calling a taxi, since I had no car and Mom and Dad lived twenty minutes away. But arriving at my parents' home at 3:30 in the morning with absolutely nothing to say seemed ridiculous.

So I sat on the tiny mattress with the thin sheet wrapped around my shoulders, and I thought about David. I mourned his passing even as his chest rose and fell, rose and fell.

As I glanced around the dark, antiseptic hospital room, my attention was caught by David's favorite items, which Loreen had carefully placed on the table beside his bed. I stared at the bright red, blue, and yellow Mexican ceramic bird with the broken nose and wondered why it was there. Next to it was a three-by-five-inch framed picture of Edward, sitting at a kitchen table wearing a black-and-red flannel bathrobe. A small stained-glass rainbow shimmered in the sunlight behind him.

I reached for two quartz crystals. I recognized the shiny, white, nearly transparent one: It had belonged to Edward, and David inherited it when Edward passed—according to Loreen, who had shown them to me the day before. The other stone was a mottled, cloudy, opaque wand about four inches long and an inch thick. It felt heavy. Loreen said David always carried it in his pocket.

Immediately I felt a warm tingling from Edward's rock. I quickly opened my hand, fumbled, and stared. The two stones lay side by side in my hand, but Edward's crystal felt warm and pleasant while David's felt cold and unresponsive. *This certainly is peculiar*, I thought.

Was I experiencing energy from Edward's crystal? I knew I'd had minimal sleep for five days while worrying about David, so maybe I was imagining things, but I could have sworn I just felt the crystal pulse. I gazed at my open palm. As a kid, I played with rocks all the time, and not once did I feel anything but rock. Loreen says crystals have energy. Maybe the energy I felt from Edward's crystal was a sign.

My dad is a retired Episcopalian minister. At the time, he still occasionally officiated at weddings and funerals. Our whole family is familiar with death because funerals, like other ceremonies and rites of passage, were such an integral part of our childhoods. Yet I couldn't remember ever speaking with my family about life after death, and we never spoke about crystals.

I didn't even believe in God, although I did believe there was a God. I just hadn't found it for myself.

I closed my hand gingerly around the crystals and again felt a comfortable vibration from Edward's. I recalled Edward's message of support in the Meditation Room. The tingling sensation from Edward's crystal seemed like a direct validation that he was there and would take care of David.

I looked at David's ashen body lying unresponsive on the hospital bed, the only sound the mechanical *whoosh* from the ventilator. It was too late to head back to Mom and Dad's, and my plan was to be with David when he passed, so I slowly moved a large plastic armchair over by his bed, stumbling a little as I sat on its unyielding seat, still clutching the crystals. I wrapped my hands around his cold, sallow fingers, only realizing later that both quartz crystals were in the center of our joined grasp. I closed my eyes, took several deep, heartfelt breaths, and sent waves of love to David.

And, with my eyes still closed, I saw water glowing with the promise of dawn, and the strange creatures holding the life energies of David and Edward swimming before me.

* * *

I barely knew what to do with myself. I looked out of David's hospital room window: It was sunrise. Orange, pink, and turquoise streaked the sky as my whole body seemed to trill with joy. I was convinced David's soul was alive, even though his body seemed dead and breathed only with the aid of a ventilator. I felt certain that David now lived in another realm of existence with Edward.

Mom and Dad were due to return to the hospital in a few hours. I could not wait to share this experience with them.

They listened quietly as I described my night. Mom remained silent, and Dad remarked that people deal with death in all sorts of ways. I felt so empowered about my spiritual interactions with David and Edward. I knew in my heart that David's spirit lived—it did not really matter to me what others thought, but frankly I was relieved neither parent said I was crazy.

David's body kept breathing. Our cousins Randy and Chris, Chris's fiancée Joelle, our sisters Jiffy and Pam, Pam's husband Bruce, Loreen, my parents, and I gathered to sing spiritual songs in David's room. Cousin Lori sent love and support in many phone calls from Maine.

Uncle Allen, Dad's older brother, and Allen's wife, Joan, arrived midafternoon. Uncle Allen rolled Aunt Joan's wheelchair into the room, and their voices joined our choir. Aunt Joan's stroke at the tender age of forty-five may have kept her wheelchair-bound, but it hadn't affected her beautiful voice. It soared as we sang rounds of love around David, voices adding harmony upon harmony, verse after verse.

It had been seven days since David entered the hospital. Dad visited David that evening by himself, and he was the last family member to see David alive on this earth. The early Sunday morning hours of October 1, 1995, claimed David's body, and he passed away peacefully in his sleep.

Jeff, Ken, and Ryan flew in from Pennsylvania, and I met them at Logan Airport, joined by my youngest sister, Jiffy, her husband, John—a police officer often called "Officer Friendly"—and their two sons, Stephen and Matt. All four young boys laughed and giggled as they ran through baggage claim, enjoying being together again.

We headed to the local mall to buy ties and white shirts for the boys as we tried to explain that Uncle David had just passed from this earth. Plans to celebrate David's life materialized.

We gathered at the funeral parlor at the end of our street. Months later, after the shock of the funeral had subsided, I would recall seeing David's face peeking around the corner of the funeral parlor's room as we greeted friends and associates, the hundreds of people who came to express their sympathy. The huge outpouring of love and support astounded David.

David's funeral was held at St. John's Episcopal Church. I sat in the front pew with the rest of my family and thought about how Dad was the minister of this church for nine years before he changed careers and became a marriage and family counselor and a primal therapist.

I have fond childhood memories of living in the rectory, our home, located right beside St. John's. Our entire family assisted Dad with his services. I played the beautiful church pipe organ; David was an acolyte; Mom and Pam sang in the church choir; and Jiffy, eleven years younger than I am and too little for any of that, went to the church nursery school.

Today, the pews were filled to celebrate David. My certainty that his soul remained alive provided me with the support I needed as we sang all four verses of "Amazing Grace."

David spent his entire career working in the restaurant industry. He advanced from dishwasher to waiter to maître d' and spent years as manager of the classy Ten Center Street restaurant in Newburyport, Massachusetts. Numerous co-workers and friends donated the food and drink for a marvelous post-funeral celebration at my parents' home, catering an awesome celebration of David's life.

During the gathering, Aunt Joan quietly shared with a few of us that the day before David passed, she had a vision of him ascending to heaven.

In the vision, Aunt Joan and David's guardian angel stood on either side of David, holding his hands as he rose. Aunt Joan eventually released her hold and watched David and his guardian angel continue to ascend on their own.

Peace and contentment graced Aunt Joan's gentle face as she described her experience. I nodded my head in understanding and wondered if her meditation practice and yearly visits to an ashram had helped facilitate her vision of David's ascension.

A week later, Loreen mentioned that the day after David's funeral she entered her bathroom at exactly 7 A.M., just like she did every day. She heard an unusual pecking noise and could not figure out its origin. She peeked under cabinets, glanced around the claw-foot bathtub, and searched behind the door. As she looked up at the skylight, she was startled to see an enormous black raven staring down at her, rapidly pecking at the glass! Bubbles, Loreen's faithful but somewhat skittish Bichon dog, was running in frenzied circles around the bathroom, screeching in terror. He finally stopped when Loreen picked up his shivering body and attempted to scare the bird away with a broom.

The next day, the raven was there again at exactly 7 A.M. And the next day, too. On the third day, Loreen began to suspect this raven held David's energy. They'd lived together for five years—he certainly knew her morning rituals.

After five days of daily raven greetings that sparked wild barks and crazed behavior from Bubbles, Loreen said to the bird, "David, I know it's you. I'm all right, but you're scaring the dog! Please go away." The raven left immediately, never to be seen again.

As Loreen shared her experience, we both shook our heads in awe, amazed that David could be so visible in so many different ways as he passed from this world. I wondered when he would appear next.

✳ *Illumination* ✳

Love is the centerpiece, the cornerstone, and the ultimate purpose of our universe.

Death can assume many shapes and forms. Our loved ones communicate with us in a variety of ways after they pass from this world.

Spiritual communication will increase if you believe it can occur, and if you want the process to continue!

Be aware of any style of communication from your loved one who has passed on. You may see something out of the ordinary or encounter an animal that seems to have the energy of your loved one. You may have an STE—Spiritually Transformative Experience[3]—where you see a vision or hear the voice of your beloved.

I encourage you to *believe* what you see or feel *if* it is comfortable for you. Thank whoever sends you a message, and share love.

If something does not feel comfortable, just send it away. With clear intention, say out loud emphatically, "I do not want this," and do not dwell on the experience.

Remember to send love. The more love we send, the more we receive.

Consider keeping a journal, especially if a person or an animal you love passes on. Record your thoughts, feelings, and any unusual occurrences. Keep an open mind. Allow yourself to receive support and sympathy from your friends and family.

Be open to the love being showered on you.

✳ *Chapter 2* ✳

Passages (NOVEMBER)

What the caterpillar calls the end of the world,
the master calls a butterfly.

—LAO TZU

Six weeks after David's funeral, I was sitting at the kitchen table, flipping half-heartedly through *TIME* magazine. It was a peaceful Saturday morning. The sun beamed brightly through the large bay window in our kitchen. Warm golden light cast a luminous glow on our acre of meadow. Stream-side trees swayed softly in the gentle wind at the back edge of our yard.

Jeff stood at the kitchen sink, washing dishes after his special homemade chocolate-chip pancake breakfast. Real maple syrup from Vermont was the highlight of our family treat. Jeff's previous work in the lumber industry had taught us the value of this natural sweetener. He and Ryan drizzled their syrup carefully, while Ken and I sloshed it all over our stack of pancakes. Frankly, the kids often preferred Aunt Jemima, but we always had a choice when Jeff made his morning feast.

Ken, age eight, chattered nonstop as his Lego towers grew higher and higher, soon to crash in a glorious cacophony of red, blue, and yellow plastic all over the table, each crash accompanied by cheers of joy. Ryan, age six, was absorbed by his Game Boy. The bells and whizzes of victory announced each rapidly conquered level as his head bent in quiet concentration.

I turned a page of the magazine and cried out, my body quivering in shock, tears suddenly cascading down my face.

The boys looked up from their games, alarmed. I couldn't explain what was wrong; all I could do was point with a stiff index finger.

Jeff leaned over my shoulder and studied the photograph splashed across the page.

"That's the animal you saw at the hospital, isn't it?"

I nodded yes, tears splattering onto the glossy paper.

My heart beat wildly as I rushed upstairs to retrieve the pink memo with the quick image I'd sketched at the hospital. I ran down the steps two at a time and skidded back to my chair. I placed my drawing next to the magazine photograph: It matched! The mysterious beast I'd seen was right there, photographed for *TIME*.

The animal was a manatee—a gentle sea cow that migrated in Florida.

I'd never heard of a manatee, let alone seen one. Ken and Ryan stared at my simple line drawing. Jeff read the story over my shoulder. I absorbed each word, feeling like a drowning person who has just caught a life preserver. I held on with all I had, trying to digest the implications.

What was the connection between David and manatees? Was this some kind of message?

When I first learned David was sick, we were camping on

Cape Cod with family, extended family, and friends—a reunion tradition since 1955.

David had become a bit distant in the prior few years. It was wonderful to be together again, sharing our love of the ocean, camping, and family fun.

We walked together on our favorite beach, Coast Guard, at the Cape Cod National Seashore. Seagulls soared on gentle ocean breezes, their white breasts glistening in the sun. Ocean waves crashed onto the golden shore as hundreds of pebbles tinkled back into the cold Atlantic Ocean.

David was four years younger than I, and we had always been extremely close. I loved his free spirit.

I am the oldest of four children; David was the third child and only son. I went to Utica College of Syracuse University to study occupational therapy, and a few years later went to Boston University to receive my advanced master's in the subject, graduating summa cum laude. Pam, the second-oldest, went to the Massachusetts General Hospital School of Nursing, one of the best in the nation. Jiffy, our baby sister, opted out of college and worked in the insurance industry.

David quit high school as a senior, saying all the rules and "stupid" school projects were not for him. He earned his GED the summer after his senior year, sitting on top of his summer school desk, finishing high school on his own terms. He had a perfect 4.0 GPA his final semester.

I lived in Pennsylvania, and David lived in the seafaring New England town of Newburyport. We did not see each other much except at traditional gatherings like Christmas, Thanksgiving, and the annual Cape Cod family reunion, and then only if we could both take off work at the same time. We always enjoyed sharing thoughts and talked regularly by phone, but spending time together in person was rare and special.

It was the early 1990s. There was lots of news about

thousands of people dying each month from AIDS. David partied a lot—we all did—and I hoped he was taking appropriate precautions.

That day on the beach, I asked casually, "David, have you been tested for AIDS?"

He swiveled his head away from me, looked beyond the rocky shoreline, and said nothing. I felt like a wall had slammed down between us.

I waited to hear him say that nothing was wrong, but for ten long, shuffling steps through hot, burning sand, there was only silence.

My heart beat faster and faster, spiraling into a crescendo of fear. My brain slowly processed the fact that David had not yet denied having AIDS. I almost repeated my question, but the concept of his being sick and dying was absurd. I knew he was gay, but for him to have AIDS did not seem at all fair and was therefore totally unimaginable.

I learned David was gay in 1980. He officially came out to the family when he was in his early twenties and I was twenty-six. Mom and Dad were disappointed but worked hard to understand and support him. I didn't care about his sexual orientation—I just wanted him to be happy, to be treated nicely, and to feel good about himself.

Finally, David's shoulders heaved and he said, "Yes, I have been tested. I am HIV-positive. It isn't AIDS, but it can develop into AIDS."

A cold chill penetrated every cell of my body, and I shivered despite the beating sun. My brain was having trouble processing what felt like David's death sentence. I could not fathom what I just heard.

My words came out in staccato questions. "David, are you sure you're HIV-positive? Have you been to the doctor? What do you mean, HIV-positive becomes AIDS?"

"HIV leads to AIDS. The best doctor in Boston is treating me. I am doing the best I can."

David had AIDS? My mind started to whirl into a deep, black hole as I struggled to understand. At that time, people with AIDS lived only three to four years, if they were lucky.

"How long ago did you find out?" I sputtered.

"About three years ago."

David's large brown eyes stared into mine, into my soul.

"I make sure not to be around people, especially the kids. I don't want any chance of blood getting on anyone."

I was beyond stunned. My heart felt like a shattered hourglass turned upside-down, leaving a thousand grains of sand to scatter in the wind.

"David, I am so very sorry." My eyes filled with tears that threatened to fall. I would not cry; I did not want to make a scene and embarrass him. "Is there anything I can do?" I whispered, my throat tight with disbelief and agony.

"Please don't tell anyone, Becky, not even Jeff. I don't want to be treated any differently." He turned away abruptly.

I blinked hard. I couldn't even tell my husband? This was going to be incredibly hard, but I would do anything David asked.

My breath caught as I said, "I promise, David." My feet struggled to move forward.

We turned around. The sun had sunk behind a bank of gray clouds. It would be dark soon. Dozens of colorful beach umbrellas fluttered in the frigid breeze. I shivered uncontrollably.

We walked the rest of the way back to our family in silence.

The rest of the vacation was a blur. I went through the motions but had lost my passion. I could tell, just by looking at Loreen, that she was aware of David's diagnosis and had realized that I knew, too. I struggled with silence and became silent myself.

Once we returned home, David and I talked regularly by

phone. We exchanged stories and only chatted a little about his illness.

But my heart broke a little more with each new symptom. He developed the dark skin lesions called epidemic Kaposi's sarcoma. He contracted hepatitis. His HIV turned to AIDS.

Because I had agreed to keep his diagnosis confidential, I was unable to find solace in discussing David's condition with anyone. Nothing made sense, and I began to search for some kind of meaning, some kind of answer.

Even though our dad was a minister and had his own views, I had never reached a conclusion about death that felt comfortable to me. I was desperate to find meaning in life, as I could not find the reason for David's impending death.

I found myself drawn to hundreds of books on metaphysical issues. I read about talking with "dead" people. I learned that energy is "alive" and can be readily accessed, especially in nature. I devoured nonfiction stories about people who communicated with spirits, souls, and loved ones who had passed over. I wondered whether these stories were true. I thoroughly researched each author's background and was reassured when the writer seemed "normal."

As I stood for hours in the New Age section of bookstores, learning to trust my instincts about which author to read next, numerous people approached me. We shared experiences and thoughts and recommended books to each other. My awareness about the interrelatedness of all life expanded as I searched for the meaning of life and death.

When I found an author whose views resonated with mine, such as Mary Summer Rain[4–12], Tom Brown[13–16], and Michael Roads[17–19], I read every one of their books. I wanted to experience their journeys from beginning to end, so I started with each author's first publication and continued chronologically until the most recent.

Stories of life after death and different realms of existence consumed me. I knew no one who "talked with dead people" except for authors, who began to feel like friends. Many times I questioned my willingness to believe these engrossing revelations, but I discovered that these disclosures offered me the framework of belief I desperately wanted for the continuity of life.

Books piled up on my nightstand and spilled onto the floor. Newly purchased bookshelves housed my growing collection of nonfiction depicting otherworldly experiences. I felt a glimmer of hope as I began to realize that the life most of us lead is not all that life is.

David had lived with his HIV diagnosis for three years before he shared the news with me on that transformational day on the beach. He persevered for almost four more years and was considered a long-term survivor. A few of David's closest friends knew about his condition, but until six months before he passed, I was the only family member he told.

Now, six weeks after his death, I sat at the kitchen table looking at the manatee picture, deep in thought. I recalled all the metaphysical books I'd consumed. David and I used to talk for hours about Mary Summer Rain's signature book, *Spirit Song,* her entrée into the world of metaphysics. I gave David the entire set of Mary Summer Rain books after I read them, so we were both familiar with her philosophies and concepts of other dimensional realities. I'd never read a book that described an experience like I'd had with David in the hospital, but possibly our shared experience of the books enabled us to communicate as he passed from one dimension to the next.

I continued to stare at the manatee photograph. Since David's passing, I had been lethargic, desolate, and unable to concentrate with my usual sharp focus. I frequently replayed my hospital encounter with David and Edward, wondering if I was crazy, sick with grief, and had somehow made up the whole experience. Today I tilted my head sideways, puzzling over the manatee photograph, flabbergasted to realize the vision I had seen in the hospital was a real animal.

How did manatees relate to David?

The *TIME* article noted that most people seemed oblivious to the plight of the manatee. Manatees lived just below the ocean surface, and motorboats regularly drove over them. Propellers cut and scratched their wrinkled skin, and the infected wounds eventually killed the animals. According to the article, this was why manatees were rapidly becoming extinct.

Our society had not fully addressed AIDS, the killer disease overtaking the homosexual community. That thousands of people were dying of AIDS was not commonly acknowledged.

The connection between vanishing manatees and the AIDS epidemic might seem farfetched, but it was a connection nonetheless. And the more I thought it out, the stronger it felt.

Synchronicities clicked into place. David and I both relished the ocean, loved swimming in it, always felt comfortable when we were seaside. We bodysurfed each summer, competing to see who could ride waves the farthest. He had confided in me, revealing his AIDS diagnosis, as we walked together along the ocean shore.

David lived by the sea, though he was unable to swim for the last two years of his life. The medication cocktail that sustained him entered his body through a tube inserted permanently into his stomach, which made swimming impossible. If the manatee in my hospital vision was David—and I felt certain it was—then it was clear that when David passed over, he chose to swim in his beloved ocean once again.

My mind whirled as I tried to understand. Jeff knew about the shapeshifting vision I'd had while sitting with David on his final night, but I had not talked about it with Ken or Ryan.

I picked up the pink sheet that held my simple drawing of

what I now knew was a manatee. My hands shook as I started my explanation.

"When Uncle David was dying in the hospital, I spent the night with him, since I didn't want him to die alone." Ken looked at me, his eyes brimming with tears. Ryan nodded encouragingly. Jeff laid his hand on my shoulder. I took a deep breath to steady my voice.

"It was the middle of the night, and I was all alone with Uncle David. He was hooked up to a machine that helped him breathe. I reached for Uncle David's hand and closed my eyes. Then I saw the weirdest animal I'd ever seen, swimming in the ocean."

I point to the manatee picture in *TIME*. "Somehow it felt like Uncle David's energy was inside this animal. He was really happy swimming in the ocean again. Then another manatee arrived. I think it was Edward—you remember him, Uncle David's best friend from when he was a little boy, who died last year? They seemed thrilled to be together."

I paused. "It seems like Uncle David is still alive."

The boys looked puzzled. Ken asked, "Mom, do you mean Uncle David didn't die?"

I hesitated, trying to make sense of this mystery. I looked at the manatee picture in *TIME* and glanced at the manatee picture I drew. I thought about the dozens of books I had read in the past four years that described how our souls continue to live even after our physical bodies cease to exist.

Clouds of deep confusion began to clear. Sunlight surged through our kitchen bay window, and my heart started to beat faster.

"I think Uncle David's body died, but his spirit still lives." I glanced up at Jeff. "It was the most incredible experience of my whole life."

That was enough to reassure the kids, who resumed playing. Jeff returned to the dishes.

I contemplated the magazine for a moment, then announced that I was going to the library to see what I could find on manatees. After the library, I swung by the bookstore. There were only a few titles about manatees, and I bought every one. I also discovered the Save the Manatee Club[20] and immediately sent in my first donation.

I was still stunned that the animal I saw in my hospital vision was a real creature, a live manatee. I had doubted my hospital experiences, but maybe David's soul really was alive!

* * *

A few weeks later, I decided to ride my horse, Astre, through a Christmas tree farm in Pennsylvania.

I had begun horseback riding four years earlier in an attempt to bring some balance into my life. Frequent hundred-hour work weeks were taking a toll on me. I thoroughly enjoyed growing my healthcare business, but combining it with trying to be a good mother and wife was draining.

When I was thirty-seven, severe chest pains sent me to the hospital for a full medical study. Stress, they told me, was the culprit.

I was not pleased with this diagnosis—I wished there were a physical cause, something I could fix with an operation rather than an emotional change in disposition or a radical change in lifestyle.

I tried hard to reduce my work hours to seventy to eighty per week and was relieved that my business continued to grow.

One afternoon about a year later, I got a call from one of my largest clients: They needed an occupational therapy and physical therapy budget by 8 A.M. the next day. I was just leaving for an appointment with my dentist, Richard Nelson, and decided to take the budget figures with me so I could multitask during the cleaning.

I leaned back in Dr. Nelson's chair, held my yellow note-pad high above my chest, and worked diligently on financial and operational projections as the dental hygienist moved around my outstretched arms. With my mouth wide open and the hygienist doing her best to clean my teeth, I rapidly calculated figures and scribbled them on the paper overhead. I always bite my pen tops (must be my need for constant sensory stimulation) and was a bit embarrassed to notice the chewed cap staring down at the hygienist as she advised me to take better care of my teeth. I finished the budget just as our session ended and felt quite pleased with my time management skills.

Then Dr. Nelson called me into his office and said, "Becky, I'm concerned about you. How are you feeling?"

"I'm feeling swell—business is great."

He slowly shook his head, handed me a business card, and encouraged me to visit the person listed on it.

I thanked him—I always appreciate it when medical colleagues refer me to their associates—and as I drove back to my office, I called the referral and scheduled a time to meet.

A week later, I arrived at a large brick building about forty minutes from my office. As I walked around staring at the signs, looking for my appointment, I saw "psychologist" in large block letters next to his name. "Am I at the right place?" I wondered, pulling out the business card and checking the name. Yes, Dr. Nelson had referred me to a psychologist!

Normally a psychologist does not need OT and PT, and it finally dawned on me that Dr. Nelson must have thought I was the one who needed assistance. I stood dumbfounded in the parking lot and considered cancelling my appointment. *Well, I'm already here*, I said to myself. *Might as well see what this is all about.*

I entered a dingy office and stared at the red plastic couch in the waiting room.

A tall, somewhat disheveled man of about forty-five emerged from an office.

"Rebecca? Please come in." He closed the door and gestured to a chair opposite his. "Tell me why you're here."

"My dentist sent me," I said grumpily.

"Why did your dentist ask you to come?"

I stared defiantly at the psychologist. "I thought it was to talk with you about providing occupational therapy or physical therapy. Do any of your clients ever need OT or PT?"

The psychologist looked at me blankly. After a few moments, he asked again.

"Why did your dentist recommend that you come to me?"

I sighed. *Guess I should try to get this over with as quickly as possible.* "I got a call from one of my biggest clients that they needed an OT/PT budget by 8 the next morning. My day was packed, and I'd scheduled a late-afternoon dentist appointment. It took me more than six months to allow myself a free hour for this chore—I hadn't been to the dentist in over two years, and when I finally scheduled it, I got hit with this rush budget. So I decided to multitask by taking budget figures with me."

I shrugged my shoulders, and I'm sure I smirked. "I completed my budget and had my teeth cleaned at the same time. Dr. Nelson called me into his office, asked how business was, and handed me your card. I thought you needed OT/PT services, which is why I came."

The psychologist said nothing about my multitasking skills. Instead he asked me to describe myself, my occupation, family history, and anything else I wanted to say.

I rattled off the basics: I was an occupational therapist who'd been running my own private practice for seven years; we worked with adults who have disabilities, children with special needs, and people with mental health issues; we serviced clients in home health agencies, hospitals, nursing homes, school systems, group homes, and outpatient clinics; I had a staff of eighty-plus therapists and loved to work.

Married for five years, my husband and I had two young sons. I was the oldest child of four. Dad was a minister, a primal therapist, and a marriage and family counselor. Mom stayed at home while I grew up, then went back to work when I entered ninth grade to help pay for our college educations. She used to work at the Pentagon, then became an executive administrative assistant, then a manager in the insurance industry. My parents and siblings all lived in Massachusetts and New Hampshire. I was the only one who lived in Pennsylvania. I didn't want to be bored and preferred to be busy.

All told, my life story took about ten minutes. I waited for the next question, but the psychologist just looked at me. I grew uncomfortable with the silence and began to squirm.

"What's next?"

"I'd like to try biofeedback on you."

"Biofeedback?" I crossed my arms and glared. "For what purpose? What are your goals? Why do I need biofeedback?"

The psychologist mumbled something I didn't catch and invited me into his biofeedback room to "try it out."

"What scientific research is available to justify using biofeedback on me?"

He stared at me, puzzled, waiting patiently to see what I would do.

"I am not interested," I said definitively. "Thank you for your time."

I paid the bill and shot out of the office. I had just lost three hours of productivity because it took me an hour to get to his office and, of course, I'd been early because I hate being late. What a waste of time!

Later that week, I found myself thinking about this frustrating but curious appointment. I'd known Dr. Nelson for more than ten years and trusted his judgment. Why did he send me to a psychologist? I considered contacting him, but instead decided to spend a few moments analyzing my behavior.

I loved my work, but I was a workaholic. My business was growing, but I didn't spend enough time with Jeff and the kids. I had tried running my business from home after the kids were born, but they were too much of a distraction—so we sent them to a family-run daycare and kept my business in the house. When chest pains sent me to the hospital, they were diagnosed as a symptom of stress.

Maybe it was time to consider taking better care of myself... what a novel thought. But I also knew that whatever changes I made had to fit in with my work goals.

During the next few weeks, I held numerous meetings with myself and wondered if maybe I needed a stress reliever. I thought about joining a softball league, but after four torn knee ligaments, softball did not seem the most sensible sport for my body (though I do love it). I spent a few pleasant moments reminiscing about the time our softball team won the club championship when I was in graduate school. I had torn those ligaments the night before our championship game and decorated my crutches with red satin ribbons in the BU school colors. Having colorful crutches changed my focus from disability to creativity during four months of rehabilitation.

I considered taking a painting class, but painting seemed to require a relaxed atmosphere, and I was definitely not relaxed. I thought about joining a book club, but most met at night. I was consumed with meetings three to four nights a week, along with attending Ken's and Ryan's sports and music events whenever possible. I did not need another evening commitment, and I was not going to take time away from work for a daytime book club.

I spent a month trying to figure out how to continue

growing my practice, raise a family, maintain a solid relationship with Jeff, and remain healthy. I wanted to do it all.

I relished the challenges of being an entrepreneur, the thrill of gaining new business, and the excitement of management. I loved encouraging people to follow their dreams. I also suspected that if Jeff and I had not married, I would have been dead from overwork.

I wondered, though: What were my dreams other than work? What was the purpose of my life? Why was I here? Could I keep up my incredible pace and find life satisfaction while maintaining physical health?

Finally, I started to contemplate horseback riding. As a kid at Fleur de Lis summer camp in Fitzwilliam, New Hampshire, I used to love riding horses. Maybe riding would be a relaxing and enjoyable activity for me now.

I shared my plan with David and Jeff, and they both supported my stress-relieving goal. This was probably close to the time when David was diagnosed with HIV, though it would be years before I knew he had contracted this incurable disease.

I began riding once a week on Wednesday afternoons. I worked right up until 1 P.M., when my lesson started. But I always arrived at the barn early, then sat in my car and finished up work calls for the day as I gazed longingly at the barn, my place of solace. If anyone asked, my office staff knew to say that I was working out of the office. I did not want anyone to know I was taking the afternoon off—it didn't sound professional to mention that I was taking care of myself.

I loved riding. The earthy smell of horses brought me peace. Their graceful strides were beautiful to watch. The companionship between horse and rider was soothing and relaxing. When I rode, I forgot my job immediately and submerged myself in the experience. Riding was one of the very few times I stopped thinking about work.

For three hours every Wednesday afternoon, I achieved pure joy. Within six months, I purchased my first horse.

Nicky, short for Nickelodeon, was a beautiful bay-colored quarter horse–thoroughbred combination. She was 14.3 hands high, just right for a small adult. Originally, she was owned by a youngster who kept improving her riding skills and eventually wanted a more advanced horse. I thought purchasing a "kid's horse" would be an easy riding transition for me. I was wrong—kids are often better riders than adults.

I tried hard to ride Nicky successfully, and we had a great time together. I particularly enjoyed the hour we spent outside the ring, riding by ourselves through the woods behind the barn. Nature's treasures were gloriously illuminated as we trotted through the forest, listening to birdsong and spying the occasional rabbit or fox. I savored the peace and quiet of nature, and my spirit thrived.

But my plan to relieve stress by horseback riding became subverted by my workaholism. I always want to succeed at everything, and I challenge myself constantly to excel. Nicky and I soon started competing in amateur horse shows, with moderate success.

Soon I was riding five to six days a week. I extended my day by waking up at two or three o'clock in the morning and rushing to work. After ten years, my business had grown so much that I purchased a freestanding home as an office building: Most of our 150 therapists were women, and I wanted our staff to feel comfortable in our business environment. By 7 A.M., I had already completed three to four hours of work. Each morning, I left a pile on my assistant's desk of "important to-do" dictation tapes to transcribe and a large pile of projects to complete, then headed to the barn. I arrived between 7:30 and 7:45 A.M. every business day.

I hired an excellent trainer and received weekly instruction at first, soon requesting lessons two and three times a week. I am not a natural horseback rider, but I loved learning how to ride. Frankly, I just love to learn.

When riding, I usually leaned forward after a jump—but that wasn't good, since I could easily go sailing over Nicky's head. I routinely landed on a pile of arena footing or, worse yet, manure. I could not seem to master the correct jumping posture. It wasn't easy to sit up straight, relax my seat, face forward, and sit back as we hurtled over jumps.

My trainer, Kerry Millikin (who eventually became a 1996 Olympic bronze medalist in the three-day eventing competition on her horse Out and About, affectionately called Outie), referred me to a sports psychologist. He used hypnotism to help me visualize the correct seated posture for jumps.

Each day before I rode, I found the only quiet, secluded place in the barn: one of the quaint two-stall wooden bathrooms. I sat on the closed seat, put on headphones, and listened to my own personal tape that described the posture I was trying to master. After just four sports hypnosis sessions, I showed marked improvement.

I couldn't stop grinning at the incongruity of sitting on the barn toilet seat listening to a guided imagery tape, but "Whatever it takes" has always been my motto.

I wanted to be the best rider possible. I'd long since forgotten that this was supposed to be about stress relief.

After three years, Nicky's old ankle injury resurfaced and prevented her from competing. She retired, and I gave her to a lovely couple. I purchased my dream horse and, because Kerry had moved away, changed horseback riding trainers.

Astre, which means "star" in French, was a big, beautiful Hanoverian thoroughbred horse, 16.3 hands tall; her back almost rose higher than my head. She and her previous owner had won eventing competitions—exactly what I wanted to do.

These three-part horse trials include dressage (which is similar to horse ballet), speedy cross-country jumping, and controlled show jumping in an arena.

My goal was to compete at the esteemed Radnor Hunt 3-Day event, a huge nationwide competition held about thirty minutes from my home. I had a very long way to go before I could qualify for Radnor, but Astre had the skill to handle it. I just needed to learn to ride her.

The day after I bought Astre, she injured her right hind foot. I put my dreams of competing at Radnor on hold. We meandered through the woods, rather than cantering on the plains. I rediscovered nature's magic and enjoyed sharing peaceful moments with Astre. The sun beamed down on us as we explored the magical forests of Chester County. Yet my internal clock still shrieked, and I cringed thinking about time I was losing to prepare for competition.

Finally, after six weeks, Astre recovered and I restarted lessons three times a week. My riding posture was rigid; I rode "stiffly." The self-imposed pressure of preparing for the Radnor 3-Day was enormous. My brain was always thinking and unable to shut down. I asked myself: *Can I ever learn to relax?*

I eventually injured my back because I could not relax my spine while riding. Thanks to two herniated lumbar disks, I experienced the most intense, grueling pain of my life. As I lay in bed, unable to move, pain shot from my lower back with every breath. I wondered if I could ever compete in horse shows again.

I tried to be still, but that was not my nature. I dictated notes to my assistant from a prone position during the next three days as the pain began to wane.

I also struggled mightily thinking about Astre. If I did not use her for competition, maybe I should stop riding altogether. Astre was an incredible show horse. If I couldn't compete, should I sell her to someone who could use her special skills? It seemed a waste of her abilities to keep her if we couldn't contend at the highest level.

I could keep Astre for my own pleasure, but for what purpose? Was it right for me to spend time with her and have no goals, no competition plans, no objectives except pure pleasure and relaxation? My life was filled to the brim with self-imposed directions and responsibilities. I rarely did anything without a purpose. Why start now?

I gingerly got out of bed, went to the library, and selected half a dozen books about back pain. *Freedom from Back Pain: An Orthopedist's Self-Help Guide* by Edward A. Abraham, M.D., talked about taking control of pain with programmed relaxation: "An ability to relax at will anywhere, anytime, and under any circumstances." He wrote, "Until we can program relaxation into our lives, the stress of life continues... until our bodies reach a point of no return."[21]

Chest pains, a psychologist referral, and now severe back pain. When would I learn to take care of my body—and myself?

I gradually decided to try riding Astre again. We started at a walk. The moment I felt a twinge of back pain, I used the techniques described by Dr. Abraham.

As an occupational therapist, I was familiar with the body's musculature, physiology, and neuroanatomy, so it was easy for me to visualize my pain site. Then I breathed deeply and slowly, consciously relaxing the muscles, nerves, and bones at the site of the pain. The first time I tried these soothing methods, my shooting back pain stopped.

A huge smile stretched across my face. Wow, this actually worked! I decided to take my time learning how to reprogram my body to ride in a relaxed manner, rather than rushing forward. I breathed deeply and relaxed into the seat. This position felt comfortable, and I grinned with pleasure. I quickly realized that my back screamed in agony if I moved too fast or became stressed. The pain was now an internal sensor that would help me master my emotions.

I trumpeted my accomplishment to Jeff when I came home that evening. He was supportive but skeptical that I could visualize the pain away, and he asked if I really wanted to keep riding.

"Yes," I proclaimed. "I do."

I never give up.

After a few days of mindful practice, I could ride Astre at a walk without pain. Next I adjusted into cantering, thinking it would be easier on my back than trotting.

After a few weeks, I could walk, canter, and trot without pain. The moment I felt a twinge of back stress, I slowed down, breathed deeply, and consciously relaxed the area. The pain receded.

As I learned to manage my back pain, I was surprised to realize I enjoyed riding Astre in the peaceful forest with no clear goal or purpose in mind. But I still vacillated about keeping her.

After weeks of indecision, I finally decided to keep Astre for the joy of riding, rather than the adrenaline rush of competition. I realized I could not compete anymore; my goal of riding at Radnor was dashed. I felt selfish keeping Astre, but I tried hard to justify my need for personal relaxation.

Astre and I increased our daily walks through the woods. We breathed in sync, savoring the forest's beauty as we smelled the tingling pine sap. Birds chattered musical greetings as we silently passed under cozy natural arches formed by tree branches. We spent glorious hours alone out there, enjoying the solitude and joy of being together with nature. I was finally learning how to relax while riding.

Yet once we completed our morning trek, I hustled to

brush and groom Astre, give her a carrot, and leave her stall, checking my watch as I rushed back to work, my mind whirling with ideas, decisions, and projects.

During this same period, Jeff, who was forty, decided to change careers and become an elementary education teacher. This was a huge decision—he had worked in sales and marketing for twenty years—but teaching seemed like a terrific fit for his caring, loving demeanor, especially around children.

Jeff went to graduate school at night and took care of Ken and Ryan during the day (we saved lots of money on daycare). I continued to work my regular seventy- to eighty-hour weeks. We hired many evening sitters for the kids.

Our schedules seemed impossible, but it worked for our family. Jeff's a night owl and I'm an early riser. He studied late into the evening, enjoying the peace of a quiet household.

When I rose at 2:30 A.M. to start my day, Jeff was still up, finishing his classwork. I would silence my shrill alarm clock, check on the kids sleeping in their rooms, and dash downstairs to greet my husband with a quick kiss. I tried to get home by dinnertime every weekday, but work took precedence. Jeff always had dinner ready whether I ate with the family or not. Most weeknights he gave Ken and Ryan a bath, read them a story, and got them ready for bed. Three to four nights a week, I made it home about 9 P.M., in time to kiss the kids goodnight and hug them for a few extra moments if I'd missed their evening activities.

I always said, "Work comes first," and they seemed to understand.

Our weekends were special. I tried hard to make up for my weekday absences by spending as much time as possible with the family on the weekends. We were outside a lot. Jeff or myself—and as often as we could, both of us—attended our boys' sporting events and music recitals. The kids had a sport for every season: Marsh Creek Eagles football, basketball, baseball, soccer, and eventually lacrosse. Both of them also started playing instruments at the age of five: Ken took up the trumpet, and Ryan excelled at drums. Either Jeff or I—usually Jeff—shuttled each son to his daily events as we tried to manage our own schedules along with watching their games and performances.

But my work brain never seemed to shut off. I had a lined yellow pad of paper with me at all times for all occasions, ready to record job plans and projects.

* * *

About eight weeks after David passed, Astre and I were ambling through the woods on a crisp fall morning following our favorite forest trail, which meandered through a Christmas tree farm.

I slowly breathed in the sharp scent of winter frost. My eyes crinkled with delight at dozens of bare oak trees, their branches lined with hundreds of sparkling white icicles that cast miniature rainbows across our trail. My heart felt wide open. I was filled with joy and sang out, "Thank you, universe, for such a glorious day!"

Astre and I seemed to be all alone as we reached the center of the Christmas tree pasture. I closed my eyes in contentment.

Three feet in front of me, standing on a light-green grassy knoll, stood David!

I immediately noticed he was healthy. He looked about thirty years old and was wearing jeans, sandals, and a red-and-black plaid flannel shirt. His big, beautiful brown eyes looked directly into my soul. He smiled broadly. My eyes remained closed.

"David!" I felt questions burst from my mouth. "How are you? It's great to see you! What are you doing here? How are you feeling?"

David grinned and answered telepathically, a phenomenon I later learned was called "thought transference."

I realized speech was unnecessary: Sending messages via stream of consciousness, or "thought," was much faster than speaking with words. I sent my questions telepathically and received instantaneous answers. I shared my extreme sadness at his death, my halfhearted attempts to focus at work, my inability to understand the purpose of his passing. I absorbed his rapid-fire responses: His acceptance of the situation, his willingness to communicate, his ability to transmit unconditional love. Then we shared family updates.

I soaked up his presence and bloomed like a wilted flower returning to life. Within seconds, we had communicated all our feelings and emotions surrounding his passing. We were flushed with joy and laughter, thrilled to be together again!

This was absolutely the best thing that could have happened to me, unless David was still alive in this physical realm.

A brilliant blue sky glistened with a thousand beams of sunlight surrounding us; rays of joy penetrated my bereaved soul. I was ecstatic to be with my brother.

I looked beyond David and was flabbergasted to see dozens of people. They stood in a relaxed, semi-straight line that stretched horizontally across the right side of the same hill where David was standing. I looked more closely and realized they were the most cherished people in my life who had passed from Earth.

Closest were my maternal grandparents, Grandma and Grandpa Dole, holding hands as always. Grandpa and Grandma had always been together, and here they were again, sharing their love with me as I stared in amazement!

To their right was Edward. His lanky frame towered over Grandma and Grandpa, and his huge smile beamed at me. I grinned back, remembering the times we shared when David was in the hospital.

Beside Edward was my dear friend Holly. She had passed away suddenly in her early twenties, killed in a car accident.

During my freshman year of college, Holly asked me to be her Installing Officer when she was elected to be Worthy Advisor in the Order of the Rainbow Girls, a charitable Masonic organization I belonged to in my teens. When I had been Worthy Advisor several years before, I had thoroughly enjoyed the leadership role. But as much as I wanted to help Holly, I didn't have the time to devote to memorizing the installing script. I had to tell her I couldn't do the job, even though I felt awful about refusing her request.

But now Holly and I smiled, delighted to be together. She held no judgment about me. All my guilt, held inside for over twenty years, immediately dissipated.

Enveloped by love, I stared at the peaceful gathering that extended across the hillside. I had totally forgotten about Astre, who stood quietly underneath me, not moving. I returned my attention to David, who continued to grin widely.

I thought my heart would burst with exuberance and joy, and I laughed like a child who had just discovered the magic of ice cream for the first time.

I beamed as I started to realize the implications of David's still being alive. The concept of life continuing forever was mindboggling. I could actually see him, talk with him, and share my feelings and love. My soul trilled with happiness. I felt like a huge display of fireworks had just erupted. A crescendo of magic, sound, excitement, and pleasure radiated through me.

Beyond the gathered friends was a bright gold arch about seven feet tall. In many of the metaphysical books I'd read, visualizing an arch or a doorway typically symbolized a passageway to another realm. I expected David to walk me under the arch, but instead my diminutive Grandma Dole took me by the hand, and we skipped underneath together.

The sky turned bright fuchsia immediately after we passed under the arch. "Get oooo-ver here," shouted Gramps (my dad's father), his big booming voice filled with glee. I did not see Gramps, but I clearly heard his voice. He took my hand into his own sturdy palm. I felt myself lift off the ground, and we flew through the gorgeous fuchsia sky, leaving David and our other friends behind. All sense of time had ceased to exist; it seemed like we flew for hours. We reminisced telepathically, and I sparkled with joy.

All of a sudden, Astre moved, her feet gently clip-clopping on the snow-covered ground. My body, perched on her firm back, began to sway gently.

"Gramps, I need to get back!"

We made a wide banking turn back the way we'd come. "I will always be here," Gramps said reassuringly as the glowing arch appeared again.

I zipped through the arch and arrived at the same place where I'd begun this journey. David, Grandma and Grandpa, Edward, Holly, and all the others were in the same positions on the hill.

I could feel Astre's gait begin to pick up, and I called out, "I need to go back! Will you be here again?"

I heard a resounding chorus: "Yes! We will always be here!"

I opened my eyes and pulled back the reins to stop Astre's movement.

Wow—what an incredible experience! I laughed ecstatically.

David is alive! My grandparents are still alive! Edward and Holly have returned! Life *is* eternal!

I sat on Astre's back in the Christmas tree farm for a long time, thinking about life, death, and the afterlife. Even though I'm a preacher's kid, I had never spent much time thinking about eternity before.

I stared at my watch—only twenty minutes had passed

since I'd closed my eyes, seen these beloved people, and flown with Gramps through the brilliant sky. But it felt like I'd been gone for hours.

Those twenty minutes had changed my entire under-standing of life. My brain whirled. If life was eternal, it meant I didn't need to rush around so much, trying to accomplish all my goals and dreams in this lifetime.

If we live forever, Earth is just one of many places we expe-rience. I tingled with excitement. Eternity was a long time!

I had no doubt that David, friends, relatives, and people I didn't even know who had passed on were alive; they just lived in a different dimension. I had never understood the purpose of life, but I was filled with a new purpose of my own: I wanted to learn how to communicate with them.

None of the hundreds of metaphysical and new age books I had read since learning about David's HIV diagnosis included experiences identical to mine, but they all described spiritual transformation. I knew it was time for me to find a teacher—someone I could question who would be my mentor and my spiritual guide. But where did I need to look? How could I find someone to teach me something I could barely describe?

❊ *Illumination* ❊

Honor your feelings and experiences when someone you love passes on. (I rarely use the word "death" because I believe people live forever.)

When a person transitions from one life to another, those left behind often encounter unexpected events that do not seem real because they remind us of our loved ones. We may feel a strong emotional impact, a connectedness to our beloved in some unusual manner. Trust your instincts. Believe that your loved one can communicate with you.

Death is not forever. People can adopt forms other than human after their passage, as when David assumed the shape of a manatee and later a raven. If you feel a strong connection to an animal, or hear your loved one's name constantly on TV, or have experiences that remind you of the one who passed, acknowledge the communication by saying *thank you* and sending love.

Many people who pass on communicate during our dreams, especially at the in-between times, like dawn or dusk, sunset and sunrise. Believe what you see, hear, and experience if it feels like a message from your loved one.

Love surmounts all trauma and tragedy. Let love encompass you, and it will multiply exponentially in directions and forms you previously thought were impossible.

If you experience a vision of your loved one, believe it. We all have free will on this earth. Our loved ones do not interfere with our lives unless we ask for their presence. If you believe that spiritual experiences and visitations from loved ones are real, they will continue to occur and increase! Enjoy the magic that comes from communicating with your loved ones who have passed. Be open to the experience and accept what happens.

Enjoy the peace.

❋ *Chapter 3* ❋

Search and Find (DECEMBER)

It is your mind that creates this world.

—GAUTAMA BUDDHA

I had no idea where to find a teacher.

I went to the library but was completely clueless about where to look. I studied bulletin boards at numerous health food stores with absolutely no success. It was 1995, so there was minimal Internet search available.

Because the traditional research methods did not seem to be working, I started to trust my instincts and allowed myself to be open to all possibilities. If a potential learning opportunity presented itself, I'd ask, *Do I feel comfortable with this path?* If an avenue did not feel exactly right, I disregarded it. I didn't realize it at the time, but I was starting to become aware of my inner self.

After two months of dedicated searching for a teacher and no further contact from David, I received a visit from one of my staff, an independent contractor named Amy Carroll. I had always enjoyed Amy's work as an occupational therapist. Her sincerity, wisdom, and personal interactions were heartfelt and insightful.

She settled into the chair across from me and said, "Becky, I met a woman I think you would like to meet. She's a shaman and lives in Reading, Pennsylvania."

"You met a shaman in Reading?"

I had read about shamans but had never met one, and I wasn't actually sure what they were. The shamans in those books lived in Guatemala or Peru or some natural place like a rain forest. Reading is a small city known for coal mining and railroads. It achieved minor fame in 1935, when the game Monopoly included a card for Reading Railroad. But it seemed like an unlikely place for a shaman.

"Nancy Arael is really nice," Amy continued. "She believes everything has energy. I just saw her last week and thought you might enjoy her teachings."

I tilted my head and smiled weakly. I am very careful to keep my personal life separate from my professional life, especially with my staff, but Amy and I had become friends. We had deep discussions about psychological and sociological matters, although we'd never discussed shamans.

I looked away and wondered if I should tell Amy about David. She sat patiently while I fidgeted, my mind whirling as I reviewed the pros and cons of sharing my experiences.

I leaned forward slowly and began.

"My brother David died three months ago." I paused and took a deep breath. "I have seen David since he passed on." I looked directly into Amy's eyes. I hoped she didn't think I had lost my mind.

Amy reached for my hand; her eyes glistened with unshed tears, and her lips puffed out in sorrow. "Nancy communicates with all sorts of spirits and people who have passed on," she said.

Could Nancy be the teacher I had been searching for? My instincts clamored "yes," and I asked Amy for Nancy's phone number.

That evening, I called. The voice that answered was cheerful and upbeat. Funny—I expected her to sound soft, quiet, and demure. Her energy crackled over the phone line.

I introduced myself and explained my connection to Amy.

"Oh, yes, she mentioned you. When would you like to get together?"

My, this was going faster than anticipated. But Nancy sounded "normal," albeit a bit happier than anticipated.

I took a deep breath. "How about next Wednesday afternoon?"

I could still work a full day if I got up early and skipped my morning ride.

I hung up the phone, grinning with anticipation. I was going to meet a shaman... whatever that meant!

Jeff was standing at the kitchen sink, looking out the window while he loaded the dishwasher.

"Jeff, do you know what a shaman is?"

"Not really. Why?"

"Amy, one of my therapists, says they work with energy. She gave me the name of one, a woman who lives in Reading. I just set up a meeting for Wednesday."

Jeff scratched his head. "She lives in Reading?"

I shrugged, smiling at the absurd notion of a shaman who lived only forty-five minutes away—practically next door.

I worked extra hard all week and went to bed early Tuesday night. I jumped out of bed the next morning at 2:00 and sped downstairs to my home office. Snow was starting to fall heavily. By 10 A.M., over a foot of snow covered the ground. Huge flakes gusted from the cloudy sky. Maybe I should cancel my appointment with this shaman? No, that seemed unnecessary. I had grown up in New England and was very familiar with huge blizzards. My four-wheel-drive Suburban, the same van that pulled Astre's horse trailer, could plow through anything.

I kept looking out my small basement home office window while snow piled up. Finally it was time to leave. I called my assistant and said I was heading to a meeting. She didn't question me. I always drive in the snow and rarely cancel work, and she knew my workaholic style.

This was a real nor'easter. Driving was treacherous. My head pounded as I peered through tiny peepholes in my snow-covered windows. The wiper blades screeched over ice frozen on the windshield. I opened my driver's-side window, leaned outside, and immediately got blasted with snow as I tried to bang icicles off the ineffective wipers.

"Becky, it's really stupid to continue in this weather," I wailed out loud. I almost turned around, but giving up is not in my nature. I had worked long hours all week to take the afternoon off, gotten a good night's sleep, and risen extra early that morning. I really wanted to talk to this woman, this shaman, about my communication with David.

I continued to creep forward, barely reaching twenty miles an hour.

Suddenly, the skies cleared. The sun shone brightly. The wind ceased to roar. Snowflakes sparkled in the sunlight. The road was still covered with freshly fallen snow, but a feeling of peace overtook me, and a sense of "rightness" permeated my soul. The rest of the drive was quiet, clear, and uneventful.

I pulled up to the address Nancy had given me and peered down a long, snowy lane. A small, brightly lit house was perched at the far end. Large, dark boulders, mostly hidden by white snowdrifts, covered a small hill that cast warm shadows on the left side of the roof. Huge oak trees arched over both sides of the driveway, their branches laden with snow. An old wooden shed creaked in the wind, its front door askew.

I checked the address. *Well, this looks like the right place.* I drove slowly down the lane, captivated. Fresh snow shimmered everywhere.

As I opened the car door, a big glob of snow fell from the roof, barely missing me as my feet sunk into two feet of powder. *Thank goodness for warm winter boots,* I thought as I trudged toward the beacon of light streaming from the open door.

A woman stood in the doorway, cheerfully waving in greeting and beckoning me in. She was wearing a soft summer sundress, which didn't make sense. Long brown hair framed an ageless face filled with freckles. Somehow I did not expect a shaman, even one named Nancy who lived in Reading, to have freckles.

Nancy murmured, "Becky, it's safe here."

Safe? What in the world does that mean? I glanced over her shoulder into her home. It looked welcoming, although when Nancy used the word *safe,* I did briefly question my sanity.

I decided to trust my gut, took a deep breath, smiled, and walked inside.

I tugged off my snow-logged boots and hooked my insulated gloves, brightly colored wool hat, and navy blue down coat on the lightweight coat rack. Nancy grinned at my large pile of winter wear and asked if I'd like a cup of tea.

Tea sounded great, but instead of answering, I heard a question pop out of my mouth: "I was driving here in a major blizzard. All of a sudden, the skies cleared, the sun shone, and the snow stopped. Did that have anything to do with you?" I couldn't believe I'd asked her that!

Nancy nodded. "I was praying for your safe journey."

Somehow her answer made sense, although I had never heard of prayer changing the weather.

"It certainly worked! Once the sun came out, I had no problem. Plus, I *always* get lost but found your home without difficulty. Thank you very much!" My map-reading skills were questionable at best, and this was years before smartphones and GPS.

Nancy led me into a lovely sunny room.

Huge windows filled the left and front walls. Dozens of brightly colored stones lay on white wooden counters beneath each windowsill. Native American artifacts dotted the room. Two overstuffed chairs faced each other in front of the open door, and a small round wooden table nestled within arm's reach. A beautiful wool blanket with colorful Native American weaving and a black-and-white border covered a full-length massage table regally positioned in the center of the room. Soft winter light illuminated snow crystals peeking through the windows.

Nancy handed me a mug of caffeine-free herbal tea. I inhaled the flowery aroma; it smelled delicious.

As I settled into the chair nearest the door, Nancy asked, "What can I do for you?"

I sipped my tea and took a deep breath. *Here we go.*

I described meeting Edward in the hospital meditation room and shared my feelings of relief when Edward said he'd accompany David as he passed over. I highlighted the swimming ocean animals that seemed to hold David's and Edward's energy, and how the world seemed much brighter as I experienced David's love when his spirit entered me. I told her about Loreen's raven that came every day at 7 A.M. and left when Loreen acknowledged David and said she would be all right.

I shared my discovery of manatees in *TIME* magazine and my new clarity about the relationship between manatees and people with AIDS: Both were becoming extinct. I talked about seeing David, Edward, my grandparents, and Holly when Astre and I were riding through the Christmas tree farm.

"It's all happened in the past three months." I lifted my head and looked straight at Nancy. "I don't understand any of this, but I want to learn more."

Nancy nodded her head encouragingly and described numerous examples of her own interactions with people who had passed on. I leaned forward in my chair, astounded.

I had finally found a teacher!

Amy had encouraged me to bring a tape recorder. I asked Nancy if it would be OK to record the rest of our session.

"Of course," she said.

I slid a portable recorder from my overstuffed pocketbook and stood the four-inch device on the table beside us. It was the same one I used every day to dictate notes and thoughts while driving between therapy sessions. It maximized my time so I could treat one more client a day. My assistant transcribed the notes so I didn't need to handwrite them in the car after each session.

I pressed the start button, ready to learn.

I have always regretted not recording the first hour of that first meeting—that was when I received validation that Nancy was the teacher I needed. I simply forgot I had the Dictaphone with me. But I have a recording of each subsequent session with Nancy and thoroughly enjoyed transcribing the contents myself after each session.

Nancy began by discussing energy. I learned that seven major energy fields—chakras—reside in our bodies. Each chakra has its own color: red, orange, yellow, green, blue, indigo, and violet (the same color arc used in the Order of the Rainbow Girls, where I had met my friend Holly).

I had never thought about colors reflecting energy. I sat in rapt attention as Nancy explained that we are composed of energy, inside and outside ourselves.

I touched the middle top of my head when Nancy described

the crown chakra location; it's our center of communication, connecting us to higher realms of reality, represented by the color violet.

Moving my hand to the center of my forehead, I gently felt my third eye chakra, the primary psychic area of our body, which helps us discover who we really are. I had no idea who I was. My eyebrows rose as Nancy explained that our third eye, represented by the color indigo, helps us see visions, spirit guides, animal spirits, and Earth's different energies.

It seemed my third eye had been active lately.

Nancy explained, "You may hear people say, 'I can see right through that person.' What they are really saying is that by using their third eye, they can see the trueness of that person. They may also want to ask, 'Why am I bringing this person into my life? What lessons do I have to learn from him or her?'"

I nodded in understanding and contemplated what I might learn from people who challenge me, rather than just trying to shove them away. I always try to see the positive side of life, and this concept of discovery resonated well.

I learned that truths are spoken with our throat chakra, represented by the color blue. Throat chakra blocks—if we do not explain how we feel or let people hear what we believe— often manifest as a sore throat or laryngitis. (Sinus concerns imply that we have internal tears from crying within.) Throat disease may indicate an inability to speak truth, therefore blocking the energy flow in the throat chakra.

My eyes shone with awareness as a light blinked on in my brain. I recalled people I knew who had sinus conditions and throat issues—many of them did seem to suppress their feelings and not express them verbally.

Nancy smiled as she spoke about the heart chakra, colored green. It seemed strange to think of our heart chakra as green and not red.

"Our heart is the center of humanity, the center of emotions. The heart chakra makes us special and unique among beings. Love arises from our heart," she assured me. "The heart is our feeling center. Some people block their hearts because of all their deep pain; they block their ability to feel."

These concepts were all new to me, but they made sense. I leaned forward in my chair, eager to hear more.

The solar plexus, represented by the color yellow and located about two inches below the belly button, is where spirits enter and leave our bodies. This chakra's power center is activated by kundalini, a string of coiled energy that sits at the base of the spine.

When I was studying to be an occupational therapist, I took human anatomy and physiology. Nancy's solar plexus description reminded me of our intestines, but I had never thought about energy associated with them. According to Nancy, this chakra is where we tend to give away our power when we present an idea to our bosses, family members, or friends who say, "You can't do that" or "It won't work." We give up our power if we stop considering the idea, even if the idea feels right.

I hoped I didn't take people's power away too much in my role as business owner. I don't like the word "boss" and always say people work *with* our company, not *for* our company. I want to empower people, not take away their power.

The sexual creative chakra, also known as the spleen or sacral chakra, is located by the body's sexual area and colored orange. Nancy described the sexual union as an act of creativity and said our creativeness comes from this chakra. I was a little puzzled by the idea of sexuality as a creative act.

The final major chakra, the base chakra, positioned in our back at the bottom of our spine, is red. It helps us stay grounded and connected to the earth.

I have always felt very rooted to the earth and had never considered this sensation to be anything other than the physicality we experience in this realm. But when I thought about David's passage and all the events that had occurred in the past few months, I realized there was much more to life than I had ever imagined.

Nancy's hand moved in the shape of an arc. "Starting at the red base chakra, all the colors of the rainbow have been represented—red, orange, yellow, green, blue, indigo, and violet—making the chakra colors an easy image to remember."[22]

Colors weren't the only indicators of chakras, Nancy continued. "Each energy chakra resonates with tones, somewhat like the music scale."

I love music and tones. Music has always been part of my life. I took piano lessons for twelve years and organ lessons for six, and I was a church organist from ninth grade through my senior year of high school. When my parents were growing up, Mom played the clarinet and Dad played—and still plays—the trombone. My parents had been back-door neighbors since the sixth grade and dated throughout high school and college—they love sharing memories of making music together in the Wellesley Middle School and High School bands.

David played the trombone, and Pam taught herself to play the banjo incredibly well.

Ryan has played the drums since age five. We gave him his first drum set—a hand-me-down from Aunt Claudia, Jeff's sister—when he was in the second grade. We hid the drum set in the back of our Dodge Caravan as we drove to Boston for the annual Christmas gathering at my parents' home. Ryan was thrilled when we removed the sheet covering his "big present" on Christmas morning. He still plays two to three nights a week.

Ken began playing the trumpet in kindergarten. And Jeff creates beautiful soothing music on his large collection of Native American flutes, especially before bedtime.

My familiarity with music helped me feel comfortable; music and rhythm are understandable. I leaned back in the overstuffed chair and took a sip of my now lukewarm tea.

Each chakra, Nancy said, has a note associated with it, and each note corresponds with the major scale on a piano. All the major piano notes are represented in the chakras in an ascending scale.

The base chakra resonates with the C tone, the sexual creative (spleen) chakra pulses with D, the solar plexus chimes with E, the heart chakra representing love aligns with F, the throat reverberates with G, the third eye sings with A, and the final major chakra—the crown chakra on the top of our head—rings with B.

Nancy explained that energy moves primarily in a clockwise direction in a circular spiral. Counterclockwise energy movement usually indicates confusion. Energy that does not move, or barely moves, is attributed to blockage.

"Blocking the crown chakra can cause negative ideas, which manifest as headaches. Headaches can be caused by negative thoughts that we are unable to eliminate. Energy does not flow smoothly," she pointed out, "when there is negativity or a blockage."

I had always had headaches. My first migraine hit at age five; I remember lying on the cool bathroom floor at home, trying to make the pain go away.

My tea forgotten, I sputtered, "I always get a splitting headache on the first three to four days of vacation."

Nancy looked me seriously in the eyes for a long moment. "It could be something subconsciously saying you should not be on vacation."

A sparkle of awareness flashed. I knew my headaches weren't caused by caffeine withdrawal—I'd stopped drinking coffee years ago, when I realized I'd been having too much and would fall asleep during dinner. I always felt guilty when I left the office for vacation. Maybe that guilt caused my vacation headaches. If I could give myself permission to truly leave work and take a break, maybe my vacation headaches would stop. I smiled hesitantly—this was a concept worth considering.

Nancy also talked about the dark side and the light side, the yin and the yang of energy. One person can have an idea and think it wonderful, and another person can have the same idea and think it ugly. Energy responds to our perception.

"How can we have light without darkness?" she asked, her voice animated. "Unfortunately, people see darkness as more powerful than light. Light is knowledge. When you are in the light, you are more knowledgeable. That's called enlightenment. If we do not apply this knowledge about light and enlightenment to our own life, we remain in darkness. Enlightened beings are lighter, happier, more fulfilled, and more successful because they feel comfortable with their own being, their body, mind, and spirit.

"When we become enlightened, we become more connected to who we really are. We use every particle of our being to become enlightened. We do not live in darkness; we search out the light. We bring the light into our body, mind, and spirit and apply this light to our whole life. If you are fearful, angry, or in pain, you can come right out and help dissolve these feelings by recognizing this pain and dealing with it, and in the process become lighter and thus enlightened."

I was totally entranced. My days were filled with excitement, but I had no idea who I was. I constantly asked, *Why are we here on Earth? What is the function of humanity? What is my purpose in life?* I had long been searching for the meaning of existence but had uncovered no answers that enlightened me.

I became involved enthusiastically with countless projects, hoping to be fulfilled. I almost always succeeded at these projects because I worked constantly and had very high standards for achievement. I liked being busy. My worst fear was boredom. These accomplishments helped me feel successful. At some point, though, I realized I was happy but not content.

About six months earlier, I had read that once a person becomes spiritually alert, they will never be bored. I thought, *Spiritual enlightenment is for me!* But I had no idea how to become aware.

"We have to ask for assistance," Nancy said. "Our spirit guides or guardian angels are always with us, but we must ask for their help. They cannot do anything without our permission. It's just like the adage 'Ask, and you shall receive.'

"Every morning, I pray and visualize the person I am praying for that day. When you were coming, I saw the energy connected to your name and prayed for you by visualizing your energy.

"I always pray for the earth, because the earth needs to be healed. As we heal ourselves, our own energy becomes purer, and thus we heal the earth simultaneously. Since energy is both within us and outside of us, all the energy around us becomes healing energy.

"Think about walking into a room and notice who is drawn to you. When you become more healed, most people will be drawn to you automatically, although some people will be repelled by your energy if they do not want to be healed or if they are uncomfortable with themselves. People have two choices. They can either rise to your energy level, which you will help them do just by being you, or they will leave you because they are not comfortable surrounding themselves with this higher light.

"As people heal, their energy becomes uplifting, lighter, and it resounds at a higher frequency. As people move into a more healing space, it becomes difficult for them to be around people who are consumed with negative energy and refuse to be healed.

"Sometimes it's time to weed the garden. We need to weed our emotional gardens to experience the resulting beauty. Some people are just energy seekers who like to pull the weeds but not create for themselves. I want to strive to be the flower, drawing upon energy while simultaneously creating beauty."

I nodded, my heart pounding with excitement.

"Nancy, I have a friend who seems to suck away my energy each time we see each other. I am always drained afterward."

"Your friend, unfortunately, is what we call an energy vampire. People who do not know how to create energy for themselves, or do not know how to tap into their own energy, try to take energy away from others. That is the only way they can feel good about themselves. Your friend may not realize why she needs this energy, but she knows you make her feel good. You realize she feels better when she is with you, so you continue to spend time together, but simultaneously you deplete your own energy resources."

I sighed deeply. "I have really enjoyed being friends with her, but it's so draining. As you were discussing energy, I was thinking that if I don't resolve our relationship, my energy and spiritual awareness will diminish."

Nancy smiled. "It sounds like you have already learned the lesson that it is all right to pull away from this person. Most lessons are very simple. You have just learned to set boundaries."

I took a deep breath. It was going to be very hard to pull away from my longtime friend. I may have learned this lesson, but implementing it would be very challenging.

"Growing up, we are often told it is better to give than receive," Nancy said. "We are encouraged to help the bird with the broken wing. Sometimes, though, birds that have broken wings like to be pampered. They like all the attention. They do not learn how to fly, even though you know they can.

"Another way to look at the situation is that when you

spend so much time helping a person fly who does not want to fly, you have less time for others who may be more willing to be helped. Once you recognize this energy-depleting scenario, you can stop the energy drain and move on to someone who is reaching out toward you."

Intellectually, I understood what she was saying. Emotionally—that was another story entirely.

"Sometime the hardest thing we can do as givers is to pull away," Nancy said. "Givers can get drained if we do not receive because the energy flow will be blocked."

All this information about energy, chakras, and tones made sense to me. I wanted to understand the yin and the yang and how to give and receive, rather than just give. I wanted to more fully grasp the way concepts move in harmony with one another. The flow of energy, the dance of life, all spiraling in synchronized agreement with the universe, sounded magical. But I wondered: How did all this new information relate to David?

Before I could ask, Nancy said, "We are now going to do some energy work. As I work with your energy, sometimes I receive information that I will give you. I just flow with it all. If you have any questions, let me know."

Great! I couldn't wait to experience my own energy! This was going to be interesting. We both stood up, and Nancy asked me to take my shoes off because it would allow me to feel the energy of Mother Earth more easily.

I have always been sensitive about my feet.

"Nancy, can you cure smelly feet?" I blurted out. My face turned scarlet. I could not believe I'd just asked Nancy about my feet. I must be heading off the deep end of reality.

Nancy explained that there were a number of energy centers in my feet, and she would work on them as we did our energy work. I was still shocked at my audacity, but if she could help cure my foot odor in the process, it would be awesome.

I looked down at what I was wearing: navy wool pants, a dark green cotton turtleneck, a multicolored heavy cotton sweater, and warm wool socks. Nancy said energy traveled through everything, so I guessed this outfit was OK for energy work.

I moved closer as she reached toward the massage table. She gently lifted up a number of small, colorful rocks lying in front of the table pillow, each stone one to two inches long.

"I will put these crystals on your chakras to help open up your energy flow. This morning, before you arrived, I spoke to your spirit guides and asked them for guidance. They told me which crystals to use for your healing and where they should be placed."

My eyes widened. *Nancy talked with my spirit guides this morning?* A million questions bubbled up, but I tried to relax, be patient, and just receive.

"This crystal is calcite." She held out an irregularly shaped, jagged white stone with shades of blue. "And the other"—a polished, round pink rock rested in her palm—"is rose quartz."

I carefully picked up both rocks and immediately felt a warm glow spread through my body, particularly in my hands. The tingling was similar to what I felt when I picked up Edward's crystal in David's hospital room.

"I am going to place these crystals on your crown chakra. There is turmoil in your crown chakra. You need to calm the turmoil, which will be helped by the calcite. The rose quartz helps you love yourself."

I agreed that my mind swirled with turbulence. David's passage had shaken me to the core. He was a great fellow: fun, caring, loved by family and friends. I truly did not understand the meaning of his death. And I had no idea how to love myself.

Nancy lifted up a shiny blue stone with white speckles. "This crystal is sodalite and will be placed on your throat chakra. Sodalite helps you make major decisions that will soon

come up. Hard decisions that will mainly be spiritual decisions." I put the first two crystals back on the massage table
and reached for the next one while Nancy spoke.

"Bloodstone crystal will be placed on your heart chakra."

The bloodstone crystal was green...that was funny. I
was surprised it wasn't red like blood, but it did correspond
with the green chakra color of the heart. Synchronicities were
apparent, and I was again reassured by how comfortable I felt.

"Bloodstone is considered to have been the stone under
the cross of Christ. Blood coming down spattered the green
stone with red specks. Bloodstone is a very healing stone.
When bloodstone comes up, especially on the heart chakra,
there is some deep pain that needs to be healed."

David's passage had left me emotionally raw. Healing my
heart would definitely be helpful.

"The next crystal is citrine, which will be placed on your
solar plexus to help you deal with your power issues."

Citrine, a luminescent golden-yellow stone, shone brightly
in the sun streaming through Nancy's snow-speckled windows.

"Next comes carnelian, which will go on your sexual creative chakra. Carnelian helps with balance. Its presence suggests your creative and sexual areas are a little off-balance."

I rubbed the deep rust orange–colored carnelian crystal between my hands, immediately feeling its warmth, then
passed it back to Nancy, who placed it back on the massage
table in its original spot.

"This next stone is called the Apache's Tear, which goes
on your base chakra. It tells me you have a past life as a Native
American. In that lifetime, you were very connected to all the
Earth energies, and you want to get the feeling back."

"A past life as a Native American?" I exclaimed. My eyes
sparkled as I gazed at the smooth, shiny, charcoal-colored stone.

"Nancy, when I was twelve, my family took the trip of a

lifetime for six weeks. There were seventeen people from three families: mine, our cousin's, and a third family, the Fores, who always summered with us. We camped in pop-up trailers and tents throughout the United States, visiting many national parks. I fell in love with the topography and wide-open space of the Badlands, Yellowstone, and the Tetons, and the Native American teachings resonated especially. Back home, I promised myself I'd return to the West someday.

"The day after I finished my occupational therapy clinical fieldwork in Boston and graduated from college, I drove west and landed in Las Cruces, New Mexico. I stumbled onto something far more significant than my first job as an occupational therapist, although I didn't understand exactly what or why back then. Now I know it was the first place I ever felt 'at home.' I stayed for three incredible years."

Nancy smiled and reached for additional stones. It was clear she understood the lure of the American Southwest based on her decor.

"These two crystals are also rose quartz, the stone of love. One goes in your left hand, and one will be placed in your right hand. The rose quartz keeps the energy flowing, receiving and giving, giving and receiving."

Nancy was correct when she said I have a tendency to be a giver but do not receive as much as I need. I always enjoy giving more than receiving.

I studied the multicolored rocks on Nancy's massage table, and it registered that she had called them crystals, not rocks or stones. I asked her where she'd found them.

She encouraged me to look for rock stores close to my home. I should enter the store and allow myself to be guided to where I needed to be, pay attention to my surroundings, see what drew me, and ask myself, *Why have I been brought here? What can I learn?*

Search and Find (DECEMBER)

Nancy scooped up all the crystals and placed them in her pocket, then folded the blanket down to the bottom of the table. She matter-of-factly asked me to lie on my back on the table; I didn't need to disrobe. She turned on soft new-age background music and gently covered me up to my neck with the patterned black-and-white blanket.

I closed my eyes because Nancy said most people receive energy better that way, and I tried to relax as I listened to the soothing music.

"Becky, I am going to get myself centered." I could hear Nancy breathing deeply, slowly, calmly. I immediately felt mild tingling and soft pulsing energy at my crown chakra. I opened my eyes and saw Nancy's palms hovering about an inch above the top of my head. It seemed like energy was coming from her hands. It felt good. I quickly closed my eyes while trying to suppress an excited smile.

Nancy spoke in a confident voice. "I am getting mixed energy, kind of scattered. I will keep my hands steadily over your crown chakra and send you more energy. This will help you become more focused and centered."

The energy felt pleasant and comfortable. I realized that during the past ninety minutes, I had developed trust for Nancy and her teachings. I had never met anyone like Nancy, but her words meshed with many of my recent readings on spirituality, and they resonated with my own experiences.

"Your guardian angel is here with arms outstretched. Feel her energy hovering right above you."

My guardian angel is here? I twitched with excitement. I didn't even know I had a guardian angel! My eyes almost popped open, but I didn't want my angel to disappear. Instead I tried to feel the energy of an angel.

And... felt nothing. *How does one feel an angel?* I tried again. Nothing, no presence... but I was more relaxed than ever before. My body felt heavy while my body's energy felt light. My brain was alert, ready to analyze, sift through, throw out, or absorb, enamored with the teachings and rapidly assimilating knowledge. My breathing was slow and regular. With my eyes closed, my other senses were heightened.

Nancy placed her hands over my third eye and said my chakra was "open with low energy." As she began sending me energy, she saw birds perched and others in flight around my third eye. She asked the guides for clarification and received the message that at times my spirit soared, and other times stayed stationary. Apparently, the more I tapped into my spiritual abilities, the more I would fly in sync with my spiritual purpose. I had no idea what my spiritual purpose was, but I found it incredible that Nancy saw birds and a guardian angel. I was also glad to hear that my spirit soared some of the time.

Nancy said I had a strong throat chakra, which made sense: I do express myself and am not afraid to speak my mind. When she concentrated on my heart chakra, she detected a deep sadness. We both knew—and now felt—that my heart was heavy with David's passage. Nancy sent love to this area, and immediately the heaviness in my heart eased.

When Nancy moved her hands to my solar plexus area, she said it was "open but low on energy." My spirit lacked power, although my body appeared open, willing to take in energy to attain more spiritual strength.

I laughed when Nancy said my sexual creative chakra had lots of energy, lots of creativity, although my male/female energy needed balancing. I often feel more comfortable with men, operate in a male-dominated industry, and am the only woman in a household of three males. I did need more male/female balancing.

Nancy positioned her hands at my base chakra. "An image of a very large, beautiful tree, about two to three hundred years old, has appeared. Aged trees have lots of knowledge about feelings and Earth energies. This image is telling me that you are a very old tree, the tree of life. When you completely connect with the earth, you will realize that ancient knowledge is within you."

I love being around trees. I always built treehouses as a child and would relish having one as an adult. I spent hundreds of childhood hours in trees, climbing on limbs and scrambling up to the top to look as far as my eyes could see.

After living in New Mexico, I moved to New Orleans to teach occupational therapy at Louisiana State University. There was a beautiful nature preserve called Audubon Park close to my home in the Uptown neighborhood. Dozens of gnarly oak trees with thick low branches were spread throughout the park. After work, I occasionally spent the early evening climbing trees, watching people underneath me who had no idea I was there.

Finally, Nancy said she would check the energy in my feet.

"If you could fix my smelly feet, my whole family would be ecstatic!" I laughed again at the incongruity of a shaman working on stinky feet.

She used reflexology to get the energy flowing and said, "Our feet are the bases for standing. The feet represent our 'under-standing.' Many times we do not have under-standing about where we are or how we are supposed to be in this world. Your feet are saying you are searching for an under-standing. You are not completely connected to why you are here. Once you comprehend this, you're not going to have a problem, and the energy is just going to flow."

My feet tingled with vibration as energy waves surged up my body, beginning with my feet and traveling through my knees, which Nancy said denotes flexibility—that surprised me because of my multiple torn knee ligaments, and gave me relief because those injuries hadn't impaired the energy flow—and connecting with my chakras.

Nancy's hands moved gently over my chakras again. "Just double-checking your main chakras to make sure they don't close. Sometimes when we open chakras or give them more energy, they tend to shut down again. But there seems to be really good flow, and they are not closing at all."

I felt a gentle shift in my body as Nancy moved her hands over each of my chakras, each completion leaving me lighter and less stressed, more at peace with myself and the messages I was receiving.

I was extremely relaxed and not surprised my chakras remained open.

Nancy's voice continued its soothing, rhythmical cadence. "We are now going on a journey, kind of a guided meditation. Today we'll travel to the Upper World, which shamanically means we are going to a higher level of consciousness. Traveling to the Lower World connects us to Earth's energies. Visiting the Middle World connects us to present energies, where our lives are now and where we can see our overall life picture.

"There are all sorts of shamanic tools to help increase awareness, including soul retrievals, extractions, and dismemberments, but today we are going to journey."

This sounded exciting, but I tried to remain calm. *What type of journey will this be?*

"Breathe in slowly through your nose until your lungs are completely filled. Hold your breath to the count of three. Then release your breath very slowly through your mouth again to the count of three, until your lungs are completely empty. Do this process two more times. As you begin breathing slowly, start releasing some of the tension in your body."

I drew in a slow, deep breath. My lungs filled with air redolent with the fresh smell of herbal tea. I released the tension in my shoulders as I pushed air out of my lungs. I consciously breathed in again, feeling my whole body relax deeply. Slowly I expelled air, feeling tension release from the top of my head, then my neck, chest, hips, and legs; even my toes tingled in relaxation. One more time, I slowly and deeply took in breath and even more slowly released air. My body felt calm, centered, and open. I was ready to receive whatever this journey might offer.

"Keeping your eyes closed and, using your third eye chakra, visualize an eye in the middle of your forehead. Imagine yourself in a very familiar and safe place. It could be a room in your house, outside in your yard, maybe up on the hill with your horse. Choose a place that is very familiar and very safe. A place that makes you feel at peace.

"Using all your senses, visualize yourself in this very safe and comfortable location. Touch and feel the textures in this space, your familiar place. Smell the aromas. Hear the well-known sounds. Even taste the feeling as you breathe deeply in this safe, familiar spot."

I visualized the forest where Astre and I rode daily. We had come to a fork in the road. We chose the path leading deeper into the forest. A little glen appeared under the tree-covered canopy: a safe, protected opening warmed by the sun.

I smelled the pitch of pine and felt the warm earth under Astre's feet. The crisp forest air tasted delicious, fresh and new.

I heard Nancy's voice: "Look at the beautiful sky. See a bird flying toward you. Look at its feathered beauty and vibrant colors. Note the plumage around its head shining in the sunlight. The bird is getting closer and closer, larger and larger."

The scene unfolded. What type of bird would come? Maybe I would see a beautiful red cardinal, a majestic eagle, or a soaring hawk. My brain started to spin with thoughts. Was I totally nuts to believe I could go on a journey in my mind?

Waiting was hard. I needed to let go. I let myself sink deeper into the vision of my sacred place in the woods and tried to abandon doubt. I took a huge slow breath and released more tension from my body. I waited.

A bird spiraled slowly down from the sky.

"Watch the bird as it flies toward you. It lands right in front of you. See the magnificence of this bird as you look closely at its beauty. It gazes at you in a very loving way. Its eyes are kind and gentle."

A big black bird with shiny, peaceful golden eyes peered gently into my soul. I connected with this bird at a deep primal level.

Nancy had said each person has a different messenger bird or animal, depending on their spiritual needs. No judgment was implied. The messenger would be right for each person.

I bowed to my raven messenger. All doubt was erased, and I immersed myself fully in this journey.

"Its mind beckons you to walk across its wings and sit. Feel the strength of its body underneath you. Feel the warmth as you sit down on its back. Reach over and caress the feathers in your hands as you hold on tight."

I lifted my leg to sit astride the bird's firm back and wrapped my arms around its neck. My hands sank into soft black feathers that warmed my soul. I felt comforted and supported.

"Its head turns, checking to make sure you are safe and secure. Now the wings flap, and off it goes. You have nothing to fear. Just experience the flight and the freedom. Feel the breeze on your face and body. Look at the beauty of the earth below. You have no limitations and no attachments. Just feel free as you soar higher and higher, going up above the earth's atmosphere. You are safe and you are free. You are climbing above the clouds and beyond, past the sun into space."

We ascended quickly. Wind caressed my face. I felt free,

unhurried, and unfettered as we soared above the clouds. I had no concerns. I was living in the moment. I was connected to my bird, the earth, and the sky. Love streamed through my body, flowing through my open chakras and lifting my spirit to the heavens. I soared with exhilaration and freedom. I had never been so light and relaxed.

"See the sky, the clouds, and the white stars. You are heading toward a bright light. Soar higher and higher, feel freer and freer. You are now going into the light. Experience the warmth, the familiarity. You have been here before."

I quickly realized the light was not the sun but something entirely different. I bathed in oscillating white radiant energy and became drenched in the golden glow of love. A very bright illumination appeared in the distance, and we sped toward it. Suddenly, a gigantic black hole appeared directly in front of us. My breath caught. I clenched my bird's feathers. We soared through the hole's star-lined opening and shot out the other side, surrounded by gentle, pulsing white beams of brilliance. I was stunned beyond belief. My fear and doubt immediately ceased. My breathing slowed.

Nancy's soft voice purred, "Tell me, what do you see?"

"I am now in the light. Waves of light surround me. White and golden luminescent beings without bodies are present. Three, four—no, five separate beings are here, and one is quite large."

"Can you make yourself go forward to them?"

"Yes, I can!"

"Go ahead. Allow yourself to see."

A magnificent being made of glowing white light, shaped like a man, was directly in front of me. It wore an indistinct, full-length, light-gray tunic; its facial features were unclear. I was awestruck. This was unbelievable. I felt in the presence of God.

My whole life, I had searched for God. I struggled mightily to understand the meaning of God. I remembered being thirteen years old and attending church confirmation classes. I enjoyed the church community but never understood religious dogma. I talked with Dad about my questions, and he encouraged me to wait on confirmation.

I'm a PK—a Preacher's Kid. It would be news if the minister's eldest child did not get confirmed. Dad was willing to shoulder the impact of my decision, but when I heard that the bishop of the Episcopalian church was coming to dinner at our home after confirmation, I decided my religious doubts were not strong enough to bear up under his scrutiny. I became a confirmed Episcopalian but stopped attending church when I graduated from high school.

I remembered being installed as Worthy Advisor of the Rainbow Girls in my mid-teens. One part of the pledge said I needed to believe in God. I struggled with this concept and did not know what to do. I had not found God for myself; I straddled agnosticism and atheism. I thought about resigning from the Rainbow Girls before my installation, but I loved Rainbow and tried hard to understand how to acknowledge my doubts while remaining true to the order's vows. I decided to proceed with my installation by acknowledging that others believed in God. I just had not found God for me.

Until today.

For the first time in my life, I felt God's existence.

Golden white energy emanated from the five beings of light, each clothed in the same kind of tunic. Four of them surrounded this mystical God, which radiated its own brilliance, brighter than the others.

Love, peace, and acceptance filled every part of my body and soul. I felt a knowing deep in the core of my soul. A sense of rightness. A sense of completeness.

I knelt down in front of God and bowed my head in awestruck reverence. This was the being I had searched for my whole life. The most profound experience of my life was happening right now.

God placed his hands on my head and said, "You have done well. Now smile!" For the first time, I released everything. My body, mind, and soul all coalesced into one. All the scattered pieces of my life joined into one complete package. Tears of contentment and relief trickled down my face. I felt utterly and positively at peace with God's affirmation. I felt whole.

Nancy's gentle voice prompted, "Is there anything you want to ask? Just go right ahead."

A million questions floated to the surface. I certainly did not want to bother God with them! But it seemed that this was an opportunity for clarity, and I have always been one to use opportunities when they present themselves. I decided to choose just one question, as I didn't feel worthy enough for more. I struggled a bit and hesitated. What was the one question I should ask God?

"Where do I go from here?"

Instantly I received the message, "Love yourself."

I have never loved myself. How could I love myself when I had no idea who I was? Warmth spread through my body, starting in my heart, immersing me in a comforting bath of love. I was filled with ecstasy, wisdom, and contentment.

I am the center of the universe. I am the center of MY universe. I matter. I am loved. I love.

I heard Nancy's voice in the distance. "Do you want to say anything else? You can ask more."

I permitted myself one more question. "If I allow myself these spiritual journeys, will my business, the boys, and Jeff be OK?"

God's powerful voice replied, "Yes. It is all right for you to explore different realms of existence. It is OK to spend time in nature. Your work, the kids, and Jeff will all be fine."

Joyous, I felt cleansed and awash in light. I was like a flower covered in fresh rain, iridescent and sparkling like new. I was ready.

I basked in love, peace, and companionship from God and my guardian angels. I fully accepted that the universe would provide me with whatever I needed. My work, Ken, Ryan, and Jeff would be taken care of appropriately. I would grow and learn more about spirituality, and my business would take on a life of its own. I knew without a doubt that I was on the right path.

"What do you feel right now?" Nancy asked softly as tears trickled down the sides of my face.

"I am exhausted but amazed! God and my guardian angels just gave me permission to do this spiritual work!"

"What I want you to do right now, since you feel so exhausted…"

"I do not feel exhausted!" I retracted quickly, interrupting Nancy.

"It's not good to get drained. Your heart still feels heavy. Are you continuing to see your guardian angels?"

"Yes." I beamed.

"Ask them to give you a feeling or a sense when you will know they are around."

The answer arrived before I finished asking the question.

"I will see a feather or feel a light touch on my shoulder to help me recognize their presence."

"Are you feeling a different energy at your shoulder now?"

"Yes! My right shoulder." I immediately recalled Nancy saying the right side represented femininity, which I lacked.

"Good! Visualize these beings and remember how they will be when you call on them again. Know they will always be here for you, especially since you will be working with them a lot more. After a few moments, place yourself back on the bird, and start returning to Earth."

I realized I had gained all that I needed. Nancy was right; I was ready to return.

I gazed in rapturous wonder at God and my guardian angels. My heart overflowed. I had never felt such profound love.

"Thank you," I said with sincere gratitude. "Thank you so very much."

I lifted myself onto my sturdy bird's back. We flew quickly.

"You can see the beauty of Mother Earth," said Nancy. "Fly free in the air, feel light and safe. Know you are going to do more journeying to the Upper World, and all will be fine. Life will become more fun for you, and you will become more enlightened."

We landed back on Earth. I wrapped my arms around my raven messenger and expressed sincere gratitude. I basked in relaxed wonder with all that I had received. I opened my eyes and impulsively reached up to hug Nancy.

"You did great, Becky! Your first journey."

"It was incredible! Thank you. I didn't think it was real in the beginning—I thought it was all just imagination—but you said to trust myself, and it felt so right."

Nancy looked straight into my eyes. "How can it just be imagination if you also feel it? You were there. You were really in that consciousness."

Ah, yes. I was most certainly present.

"You experienced a higher consciousness where we connect with everything. When you connect with energy, you *are* there. You are feeling energy. You are being energy. You are energy.

"The more journeys you experience, the more you trust using your third eye. You receive additional information and will start feeling comfortable with the experience. It's like anything else. Take those first steps, and trust you are on the right path. You do not need to go outside yourself anymore for confirmation or validation. You just go within, and you trust. We have everything within us that we need to survive."

I wanted to learn more. I wanted to learn how to journey on my own. I wanted to experience feelings of peace, comfort, and love again. I wanted to follow God's first message to me, "Love yourself."

But I didn't know how.

People always talked to me about my personality, and I would shake my head in bewilderment. How did they know about me when I had not even realized myself?

I would try to love myself. I would try hard to understand.

I thanked Nancy and made an appointment to return the next week. I drove home in silence. Usually I blasted the radio to keep myself entertained. This day there was no music, just memories, thoughts, and a changed belief system. Love filled my soul with gratitude.

Love myself. I was beginning to see the light.

* *Illumination* *

It is important to love ourselves. If you love yourself, you can share your love with everyone you choose.

What can you do to strengthen your love for you?

Give yourself permission to take care of yourself first. What would be good for *you*?

Allow yourself to receive.

What do you want in your life? Clearly ask the universe—and be specific. Then let go of your request and wait. Try to be patient. Observe and be mindful.

Thought has energy. Think positive, and positive events will happen. Think negative, and negativity surrounds you. Strive to be specific, and clarity will rise to the surface. The clearer you are, the better chance you have to obtain your desire. Learn to trust your instincts.

Be open to the power of LOVE.

✳ *Chapter 4* ✳

Fairy Magic (JANUARY)

Wheresoever you go, go with all your heart.
—CONFUCIUS

I replayed my experience with God over and over, wondering if it was real. A sense of rightness suffused my soul, and I felt filled with such love. It seemed irrefutable, but doubts plagued me.

That night, I dreamt about a gorgeous white dove. It soared through the air, staring at me with luminescent eyes. I sent my energy into it, longing to become one with the bird and experience the freedom of flight.

The dove turned and slowly tilted its wings as it veered toward me and gently entered my body. Its energy felt peaceful and warm, but I could not fully absorb it. I was unable to relax. I felt trapped. I woke up dismayed, remembering the joy of flight and my inability to let go. I blinked at the clock: It was 3:20 A.M., time to go to work.

Corporate strategy, marketing plans, new agency contracts, and staffing issues consumed me. Most of all, I wanted my business to provide exemplary customer service.

I always worked two to three hours in my home office before the kids rose—then I ran upstairs, checked my watch to gauge how much time I had, and greeted them with joyful smiles. The boys and I would laugh at the noisy clatter of shades being pulled up, smashing at the top of the windows and making a huge racket. Ken and Ryan always chose their own clothes with minimal help. After a quick breakfast, we bundled the boys into their majestic car seats.

Daycare was at a neighbor's house, and our respective schedules determined who dropped the kids off.

Jeff had now switched careers and was teaching economically disadvantaged kids at a city elementary school, work that brought him great satisfaction. When he did the daycare run, he took his time, played with Ken and Ryan, and did not look at the clock once.

On mornings like this one, when it was my turn to drive, there was minimal dilly-dallying. I sped to our neighbor's house, kissed the kids good-bye, and rushed off to a meeting or to my office with one eye on the clock, calculating how many hours I had left to accomplish all I wanted to do.

Currently I was working on the details of our corporate meeting coming up in a few days, in the second week of January. Each year, I gathered a small group of managers to discuss, project, and plan company goals for the next year. I always tried to mix work with pleasure: Creating efficient, collaborative, and communicative teams that got along well was an important part of my business strategy. This year, we were meeting at a lovely, secluded A-frame home in the Pocono Mountains. I set aside thoughts of dream-doves and got to work.

The day of the retreat arrived. In the late afternoon, after our workday, we drove north, traveling for two leisurely hours through the rolling hills of Pennsylvania. It felt great to be out of the office, sharing stories about our lives and families without the stress of workaday issues consuming us. We laughed often during a relaxed dinner at a cozy local restaurant. After returning to our borrowed home, we stayed outside for a few moments, marveling at hundreds of stars blinking brightly above the tree line. The crisp, cool smell of winter air wafted around us. The nighttime silence was profound.

I decided to go to bed early, leaving the other managers to fend for themselves, and woke up at 5 A.M., excited to begin our first full day of meetings. I glanced out the window, delighted to see snow-covered ground.

I rustled through my clothes and pulled out my warmest green long underwear set—my favorites, as evidenced by a hole in the knee. Brown corduroy pants slipped over the long johns, a toasty (if slightly snug) second layer. My dark blue cotton turtleneck shirt fit nicely over the warm top. Next I reached for my heavy white-and-turquoise wool sweater from Sweden, a gift from Mom and Dad. Then I wiggled my toes into the warmth of navy blue SmartWool padded socks, pulled on bright red snow pants, and shoved my feet into furry UGG snow boots. I waddled over to my knee-length down coat, maneuvered into it, and, for the finishing touch, tucked my favorite hat—red and blue with a springy tassel on top—tightly into place. Yes, I hate being cold!

My bedroom door opened directly to the outside. I turned the latch, trying to be quiet, and was greeted by air so cold, I thought my lungs would crackle. I glanced at the thermometer above the porch railing—seventeen degrees Fahrenheit.

It was nearly dawn, the sun still hidden. Steam rose off the frozen lake in front of our wooden home. Bits of moisture crystallizing in the air created a mystical haze that covered the earth.

A venerable walnut tree graced the right side of the beach.

One lone branch, with a gentle slope perfect for sitting, over-hung the frozen lake. I stared at the tree, still covered with leaves, and pondered. It sure would be pleasant to sit on the branch for a minute. I looked around. No one was there. I wrestled with myself for a moment, wondering if I could allow myself to feel like a kid again, sitting in a tree. Or should I organize my thoughts to lead our corporate retreat?

I took a deep breath and trudged over to the tree, my boots crunching on snow crust. I tentatively patted the branch. It was sturdy and solid. I cautiously lowered myself onto the limb and grinned. This felt great!

The tree stood like a proud guardian in front of a grove of pine trees, their pungent smell wafting in from all directions as I carefully scooted down the branch until I sat directly over the lake. I grew up in New England, and we used to skate on frozen ponds all winter. The ice on this lake looked safe and thoroughly frozen. If I fell off the branch, I'd be OK.

I gently swung my legs back and forth, thrilled to be by myself, warm and comfortable, all bundled up in the middle of winter, surrounded by nature's beauty. I started to take slow, deep breaths, as I had with Nancy a few days ago. My body relaxed, and my mind became fully engrossed in this moment.

I stretched out on the limb, lying facedown. The bark felt inviting, its gnarly texture comfortable. My eyes closed.

I became immersed in the tree. I oozed into the bark and submerged myself in its deepest recesses. I felt brown, sugary sap move slowly through this ancient sentinel. The sap had a pulse, a beat; it knew which direction to move as it traveled through veins, aware of its purpose to provide sweet, life-gen-erating food for the tree, birds, and insects. I transformed into soft, golden bubbles of thick sap as I inched through the center of the tree like a slow-moving caterpillar on a mission. Time had no meaning, and I nestled in the tree's heart.

After a while, I slowly opened my eyes. The winter kaleidoscope of colors was mesmerizing. I basked in the comfort of transformation and shape-shifting. I looked casually at the frozen ice in front of me. I wondered... could I send my energy into the lake?

I closed my eyes again and breathed deeply from my core, feeling my solar plexus power center expand while my heart remained wide open. I felt the ice break into tiny molecules, surprised at its light and airy feel. I cracked into a hundred tiny streams of icy particles that sheared off from the center. My ears sizzled with the pop of frosty molecules shattering while my body lurched quietly with infinitesimal detonations. I had become the ice.

A fish appeared at the very bottom of the lake. I slowly shifted my focus and felt thick, almost solid water slide through my gills. My mouth formed a wide circle, and I breathed in concert with this twelve-inch largemouth bass. I stayed transformed as a bass for a long time, enjoying the freedom of gliding in the dense water. I had no awareness of anything except the present moment. I was not cold. I had no plan. I was content to just be.

Some time later, I started to feel pulled to the left side of the beach. I disregarded this call for a long time. I was thoroughly enjoying wallowing in the frigid water as a fish. But soon this pull became so dominant that I had to pay attention. Very slowly, I moved my awareness away.

"Thank you, fish, for letting me experience your reality," I said lovingly in my mind. "Thank you, ice, for showing me your cracks and letting me experience how you provide life-giving air to fish and other creatures that live in the lake."

I returned to my human body and sat up gently, feeling profoundly grateful as I reflected on the morning's magic. The sense of oneness and connectedness with nature had left me breathless.

The need to walk over to the left side of the beach kept getting stronger. Still in a daze, I opened my eyes, clambered down from the limb, and bowed to the tree in grateful appreciation.

I ambled across the beach, listening, but I was not sure what was calling me. A circle of stones, each roughly one to two feet in circumference, came into view. This seemed to be where I was supposed to be. I looked at each stone and was drawn to sit down on the largest rock, facing the water.

Immediately I felt a connection, a tiny pulse from the small boulder. I slowly closed my eyes and took several deep breaths, each more absorbing and longer than the last. I bowed my head as my body folded inward, and I quickly became immersed in the stone. I was bent over with my head resting on my ankles, my forehead practically touching the frozen beach. Normally I can't even touch my toes with my fingertips.

My heart was wide open, and I quickly felt the essence of rock. I was thunderstruck by the intensity of energy emanating from this stone. The pulsations from a few crystals at Nancy's had been remarkable, but nothing like the profound awareness that occurred with this beachfront boulder.

I realized all stones were alive, and each had its own power. I thought about all the times I had casually picked up a rock and flung it away without asking its permission. I used to love skipping rocks on the water, especially when we went to Cape Cod. I've picked up hundreds of stones, time and again removing them from their location, trying to get as many skips as possible. Distraught, I apologized and murmured, "I never knew."

I melded deeper and truly became stone. I saw the metamorphosis that rocks experienced thousands of years ago when volcanoes dominated the earth. I luxuriated in the rock energy.

All of a sudden, a shrill whistle pierced the silence.

A tiny part of my brain realized I was hearing a human whistle. From the deepest recesses of my being, I dredged up my humanity.

It was probably Bob DiSciullo, my former chief financial officer and now president, out for his morning run. Oh my gosh—the whistle sounded as if it were coming closer. I really should get up. It wouldn't be good for Bob to see me as a rock!

Despite my concern about being discovered, I moved lethargically. Rocks are ancient. Their energy is ponderous, slow, and deep. "Thank you, rock, so very much, for sharing your essence with me. I will never pick up a rock again without asking permission."

Gradually I lifted my head past my ankles, knees, and hips, and stood up facing the water. At the same moment, as the sun burst over the horizon, a green flash shot out of the stone.

"Hi, Becky! What are you doing?" asked Bob, smiling. I stared at him, startled. Bob had on dark blue tights, a wool cap, shorts, and a lightweight winter jacket. He looked perky and quite refreshed.

My brain was having tremendous difficulty moving from being a rock to talking like a human again. "Just hanging out on the beach," I stammered. "What are you doing?"

"Five-mile run around the lake. First meeting still on for 9 A.M.?"

"Sure!" I sputtered. "What time is it?" I had totally forgotten about the meeting I was supposed to lead!

"8:40."

Oh my... I had been outside in the middle of winter, essentially motionless, experiencing the essence of trees, sap, ice, fish, and now rock for hours! And only twenty minutes until I launched the first full workday of our retreat.

I gave Bob a lopsided smile. "I just need to write a few notes, and I'll be ready."

As Bob jogged toward the house, I turned and faced the lake once more. I could barely comprehend what I had experienced. "Thank you so much for an incredible morning," I said silently. "Thank you!"

I traipsed back to my room, immersed in thought.

Nancy had suggested I keep a journal. I wanted to record my morning's adventures before corporate strategy overtook my soul.

I headed to my room and closed the door. I quickly jotted down notes about my experience in the tree, feeling its life force and the slow, ponderous movement of sap. I described the crackle of tiny fissures of ice and the incredible majesty of the fish breathing through its gills as it swam slowly through the frozen water.

As I wrote about the profound experience of being rock, I began to illustrate the experience, drawing rapidly on the left side of my notebook. Then I gasped as I looked at my drawing.

A tall, skinny, elfin figure with a large triangular cap and a comical grin stared at me. The figure had a long, pointy nose, striped socks, and pointed shoes that curled up at the toes. I stared at the sketch, delighted but puzzled. Why in the world had I drawn a fairy?

I recalled the green flash when I stood up to greet Bob. My mouth dropped open in disbelief.

The fairy must have been the flash of color that flew from the rock and shot toward the horizon the moment the sun rose. *A fairy?*

I laughed in ecstasy and shock. Fairies are real! *Wowee kazowee!* I looked at my drawing again. I could not believe I had just drawn a fairy!

I quickly thought about my favorite series of books, JRR Tolkien's *The Hobbit*[23] and *The Lord of the Rings*[24-26]. My curiosity about the existence of hobbits, fairies, elves, and gnomes had just been satisfied!

Again I stared at my sketch, recognizing that my mind

hadn't been able to make sense of what I'd seen that morning. The act of journaling allowed me to process the experience and record the image of what I saw but did not initially comprehend.

I leaned back in my chair and grinned. Fairies were real!

I glanced at my watch. It was 8:55, and I needed to open the retreat in five minutes. I hurriedly changed clothes, scooped up my briefcase and yellow writing pads, strutted into the dining room, and cheerfully started our meeting.

The retreat days flew by. I felt like I had two minds: one processed corporate data, personnel issues, and financial plans while the other kept returning to fairies. What if fairies were real? Did I really see a fairy? Could I meet one again? How do they interact with humans? Did I draw an actual fairy? I actually sketched a fairy!

My mind kept switching gears from corporate growth to fairies, business strategies to fairies, marketing tactics to fairies. The juxtaposition was so great that it was practically beyond belief, yet I felt more refreshed, clearheaded, excited, and challenged than ever.

The retreat was a rousing success. We accomplished all our goals and established firm plans for the coming year. As I began to get into the car to drive back home, I glanced at my companions and said, "I want a few minutes by myself, please."

I was filled with gratitude for the incredible gift of transformation that I had received. I walked to the front of the beautiful A-frame, spread my hands wide, and, from the very center of my heart, I thanked the trees, lake, ice, fish, rocks, and especially the fairy for allowing me to experience them.

I returned home and shared my news with Jeff, who accepted all of it with support, love, and—not surprisingly—some skepticism.

I could not wait to see Nancy and tell her what had happened. As I walked into her home a few days later—it was only my second visit—she greeted me with, "I see you have met the fairies!"

I gaped at her in disbelief. "How did you know?"

"They are all over you, Becky! At least twenty to thirty fairies are clinging to you!"

My eyes practically popped out of my head. This was incredible! I hadn't said a word yet to Nancy about my experience, yet she could see fairies all over me. This was an amazing validation that fairies *are* real, and that I really had seen one.

Nancy cocked her head and grinned. "You should teach people how to see the fairies. Why don't you provide a workshop for folks on fairy communication?"

"Oh, sure, Nancy. People will think I'm totally nuts!"

"Think about it, Becky. You offer workshops all the time. You would be great!"

I shook my head in disbelief at the concept of sharing my experience publicly and emphatically said no, I had a business to run. But my heart beat in ecstatic wonder that I had really and truly seen a fairy.

Fifteen years later, I began teaching people how to talk with fairies.

❊ *Illumination* ❊

Each of us controls our own destiny and has the free will to decide our own reality.

If you find the experiences in the past two chapters interesting, consider meditation or shamanic journeying[27], which is a form of meditation. Meditation expands our minds. Both forms can give you a sense of timelessness and an ability to transcend what we consider "normal" reality.

Traditionally you will feel a deep peace, a comfort, an awareness that you can become one with the universe. It took me four months to realize that closing my eyes and breathing deeply was actually a form of meditation. With shamanic journeying, you will have your own adventures that are personally relevant for you.

Find a comfortable place to meditate in your home or (preferably) outside, beside a favorite tree.

Give yourself the gift of spending time with nature, and you will be rewarded beyond all expectations. Nature is healing and helps us relax. Enjoy the trees, the sun, the grass, the wind, and the rain.

Imagine yourself surrounded by white light. Ask for your highest good to be with you. Close your eyes and take three slow, deep, cleansing breaths. Keep breathing slowly and evenly. Be aware. Acknowledge what you are feeling. If it feels good, give thanks and enjoy the experience.

If it does not feel good or comfortable, I prefer to send it away, visualize its disappearance, and not dwell on the negative. You can always open your eyes to stop the journey. Remember to keep breathing deeply and slowly.

If you want to gain more insight, work with a shaman, spiritual teacher, or metaphysical counselor to assist you.

There are all kinds of ways to meditate, and classes on meditation are widely available. Check your local YMCA, the bulletin boards at health food stores, wellness centers, and online to find meditation or shamanic resources close to you.

There is no right way or wrong way to meditate. Choose the method that works best for you. Follow your heart. Follow your intuition. Trust yourself. You will choose the most appropriate method for learning. If one way does not feel right, learn from the experience and move on until you are comfortable and satisfied that you have found your way.

And regarding the fairy realm... fairies are real. They are fun, happy, and ready to be acknowledged. Believe that fairies are real, and they will come.

✻ *Chapter 5* ✻

Crystal Energy and
Animal Wisdom (FEBRUARY)

At the center of your being, you have the answer:
You know who you are, and you know what you want.

—LAO TZU

In my ongoing determination to balance my life better, I maintained my horseback-riding schedule. I always rode alone, just Astre and me, wandering in silence for miles through the woods near her barn. Through practice and familiarity, my rides were becoming more peaceful and contemplative. I was able to relax more and simply to enjoy being in this place at this time.

Perhaps that's why on one particular morning, when a doe leaped gracefully through the dense forest just ahead of us, I didn't startle. Instead I watched the doe's fluid movements in awe, aware of Astre's bright eyes capturing every flicker, every bound.

Can I shape-shift into a deer?

I relaxed my body, slumped deep into my Passier saddle, and closed my eyes. Astre felt my relaxation and stopped walking, her strong neck muscles flexing as she lowered her head toward the earth, her large frame relaxing with me.

I sent my energy into the beautiful deer. I visualized her three-foot height, golden-brown fur, and small dark-brown hoofs scampering through the forest, her flash of a white tail twitching, erect. I breathed in the same warm air as the deer and suddenly felt myself leaping alongside her, imitating her movements, and as my spirit soared, I merged with the doe.

Practically weightless, we jumped nimbly over logs strewn across our path, scattering dew-dampened leaves as we landed. I felt graceful—a new experience for me. "Graceful" had never been used to describe my gangly movements. Athletic and filled with enthusiasm, yes, but definitely not graceful.

Abruptly, the doe veered right, catching me unawares. I don't know why we turned, but my bond with her quickly lessened.

Rather than regret the impending disconnection, I was filled with gratitude, and before we separated, I expressed my thanks to the deer for letting me experience freedom and the ecstasy of such effortless movement.

I took a deep, full-bodied breath, starting from the very center of my solar plexus, the muscles slightly below my belly button contracting as my breath expanded and rose to my chest, my heart soaring with love. My throat widened as my mouth dropped open, and I inhaled love for the doe, nature, Astre, the forest, and all life. I exhaled slowly and sank into the relaxed flow of deep breathing. Then another immense inhale, followed by a calm and peaceful exhale, while I gradually opened my eyes.

The ground shimmered with iridescent, vibrant greens

and nut browns so vivid that they gleamed. The doe was long gone, but I still felt her in me. I was enveloped by a haze of love, peacefulness, and contentment.

Astre noticed that I was more alert and lifted her head, stretching her neck elegantly. I straightened back up in the saddle and raised the reins, and we ambled forward.

Further along, I decided to send my energy into the trees. The diversity of timber was astounding! I had assumed that all trees were the same, but even trees in the same species felt different. Most wood had energy that was warm and inviting, but some trees felt cold and withdrawn. I soon learned to discriminate between the two, remaining with timber that appeared open to my energy and quickly passing by those that felt closed.

Throughout this experience, I was filled with gratitude for the diversity and depth of my life experiences. I realized that humans are not the only entities on this earth with thought and energy. Everything—animals, birds, trees, rocks, crystals, rainbows, the sun, moon, ice, *all* natural items—have their own unique energy patterns. For the first time in my life, I realized we are never alone. What a blessing to learn how to tap into this energy stream!

I sent my energy soaring skyward with the doves, wanting to enjoy the sensation of flight today, rather than pushing myself to search for meaning.

Don't look for anything. Just go with the flow, said the flock leader.

But I can't—

But how—

I never went with the flow. I always orchestrated my life the way I wanted it. I wasn't even sure what "go with the flow" meant. How could it be possible when I had a business to run and a family to raise and—

Was this a tiny glimmer of a new way for me to relax? A way for me to be open to the magic in life, a hint of how to allow myself to experience the wonder of the universe?

At a follow-up session with Nancy, when I told her about this experience, she said, "Astre is meditating with you."

I was stunned. I never considered that a horse (even one as lovely as Astre) could meditate. I thought about sitting on Astre's back, eyes closed, slumped in my saddle, taking slow, deep breaths. I realized that Astre had relaxed too, and her breathing had slowed. Nancy was right: Astre and I were meditating together. Unsure if this discovery had anything to do with "flow"—and definitely clueless about how going with the flow could be possible for me—I described another experience I'd had a few days before, also while riding Astre.

We were deep in the woods as large flakes of snow began falling from the overcast sky. We came to a clearing in the forest that seemed to be vibrating. I felt a tremendous surge of energy; the entire space seemed filled with power. I had read that if I talked to spirits, sometimes I could create even more power, and I decided to try it: I thanked the spirits for this remarkable power spot and asked them to come to me.

A huge force slammed into me. My spirit body ended up on the ground, although my physical body still sat on Astre. Snow began falling heavily. I quickly looked to each side, disoriented, trying to discover why I was sitting on the snow-covered forest floor. After a quick assessment, I realized I felt comfortable and peaceful.

I looked up at the sun and, with a gigantic whoosh, fell into the center of the earth.

I stood before a roaring fire. Without warning, a tidal wave flooded the area and transported me to a land of the dinosaurs. I experienced a sense of déjà vu.

My favorite toy as a kid was a gray plastic Tyrannosaurus

rex about five inches long. I never wanted any dolls and was quite content playing with my dinosaur, climbing trees, cavorting in the stream beside our home, and building tree houses with my own toolbox.

The land of dinosaurs I'd just arrived in didn't look anything like my childhood backyard, but I was sure I had been here before. The earth was covered with huge boulders, spread across a flat, gray plain. I roamed above the land as if flying and reached a distant jungle where, I discovered, many dinosaurs dwelled.

First I saw a gigantic Apatosaurus, the one we used to call Brontosaurus. Next, shuddering underbrush revealed the horned head of a Stegosaurus, its massive jaws noisily crunching low-lying trees and bushes.

I looked for my favorite, Tyrannosaurus rex, king of the dinosaurs, and finally spied it far off, standing on its powerful hind legs, shaking its small, stubby arms. It swung its massive head, jaws wide open as it searched for food. I didn't come close—it was, after all, a carnivore, and I did not want to take any chances.

I didn't feel emotionally connected to any particular species of dinosaur, just simply watched them as they moved about the land. Eventually, their gigantic bodies toppled over, crashing to the earth and dying as rocky dust spewed high into the air. Soon after, I felt myself transported again. I opened my eyes and discovered that I was again in my body, settled in my saddle on Astre.

Nancy nodded as if this were the most normal event she'd ever heard about, and she asked what message I'd received from my journey.

I thought for a minute, then said, "I felt as if I were participating in one of the creations."

"So you saw yourself as a co-creator."

"A co-creator?"

She nodded. "We each create our own reality. Some of us create hell on earth, and a lot of us create heaven on earth. We create and manifest things in our lives, so we are 'co-creators.'

"When we look at the history of the earth, we realize there is a purpose and time for everything, including the dinosaurs, which you had something to do with creating. We do not know all the ramifications or why they were here, but it was very important for dinosaurs to exist and then leave."

"But—"

"Becky, when you have journeys, they don't just happen for fun. There is a meaning behind each message, a gift of knowledge and understanding for you to receive.

"You are taking the time to find out why you are here and how everything exists. When you go within, you are seeing from the inner eye." Nancy sipped her tea, then continued.

"We are universes within ourselves. We live in a three-dimensional reality that is all connected."

My whole life, I had searched for the meaning of life. What I was learning from both Nancy and my experiences while riding Astre felt right, but I was worried, too.

"Nancy, I love learning about all this, but I'm afraid of what people will think. I've tried to be careful about who I talk with about these things—I don't want anyone to think I'm crazy or a flake—but at the same time, what I'm experiencing makes so much sense, feels so right—I've never experienced the kind of calmness I'm feeling now. Yet at the same time, I find myself questioning it all."

Nancy smiled and said, "It's OK to question; that's how we learn. Eventually, we will understand what it's all about.

"If you do not feel right about something, question it. If something does not feel good, question it. You do not want to give away your power just because somebody thinks they know better than you."

"Nancy, when I shared my dinosaur experience with Jeff, he said, 'Couldn't your subconscious just be thinking about dinosaurs, and then you journeyed to the dinosaurs?' I didn't know how to answer him."

"Well, why were dinosaurs so important for you as a child? You didn't have a doll, you had a dinosaur. Everything happens for a reason. Everything is part of the divine plan and what we need to learn at the time."

I nodded my head but still doubted the validity of my experiences. "Even my journey to the land of the dinosaurs?"

"In order to heal, everything has to come to the surface. We need to heal ourselves first. Once we heal our own universe, the ripple effect spreads out to heal others and to heal the earth."

As we refilled our teacups, I asked Nancy about a comment from my friend Amy, whose recommendation had led me to Nancy. Amy had called me an *old soul*. What did that mean?

"You are definitely an old soul—someone who has been on Earth before," she explained. "Things come more easily for you than for other people because you have done this work in the past. It's also one of the reasons you doubt yourself: because this information is coming so easily. Ever since we were small, we've been told that we have to work hard at anything important. Anything that comes easily is suspect. The spiritual concepts resonated with you when you opened the spiritual door, and the door opened very easily."

It certainly had been easy. But was it real? Except for Nancy, I had never met anyone who had similar experiences. I found myself doubting my sanity often.

Yet if I were crazy, I wasn't sure I wanted to be "cured"; I actually liked this new way of thinking. I understood what I was learning, and it definitely seemed reasonable to me.

I pointed out to Nancy that all I had done was read a

few hundred books about metaphysics over the couple of years after I learned about David's illness. I believed the concepts they described were possible in an abstract way. Then David passed, and suddenly all these spiritual experiences started happening to me—and there was nothing abstract about them. And she was right, that part had been easy. But I still doubted the reality of my experiences, the things that my senses told me were happening but that the "real world" had always insisted were impossible or the rantings of a disturbed mind.

Nancy's voice was reassuring. "When we think about spiritual concepts, we are thinking about energy. Energy is thought.

"We are multidimensional beings. No one in the universe is better than anyone else. Dr. Deepak Chopra said that we are the universe, and there is only one *verse* in the song *uni-verse*.[28] Humans aren't just one note—we have many notes that create a beautiful song. Each of us resonates with our own unique tone.

"Entities like angels and nature spirits live in a different dimension, a different frequency of energy. They resonate with a higher frequency. When we tap into the frequency of other dimensions, we use psychic abilities. We do not see into the future; we tap into another dimension, another frequency.

"The door you opened by reading was the door to the universe. Since you have opened that door many times in the past, it flowed very naturally to you. Other people who have not opened the door could be frightened. Or, once they open the door, they close it right away because it's too much for them. That's why it's good to be discerning about how you approach people."

Something about this bothered me. If I couldn't share my experiences with others, what was I supposed to do? Nancy spent her time helping people get in touch with their inner beings. Shouldn't I be doing something to help others, too? It's what brought me joy in my work as an occupational therapist and business owner. Even if I wholeheartedly accepted that my spiritual experiences were real, spending so much time exploring them only for myself seemed selfish.

Nancy reminded me that we are supposed to heal ourselves, because only then can we heal others. That isn't selfish—it's necessary. When we stay focused on who we are, those around us respond to our energy, our unique note in the song. It's the ripple effect.

That's why when we walk into a room feeling good about ourselves, people respond to our positive energy. If I walk into a room feeling negative, people sense that negativity also. By allowing myself this time to heal, I would enable my energy to become more positive more often, which in turn would help heal others.

With this realization, I released years of pent-up tension and self-doubt.

I had worked hard and long my entire life and rarely relaxed. Frankly, I didn't know how to relax. Whenever space was about to open up in my schedule, I created a new project to accomplish, found two or three must-read-now books, and added to my list of urgent things that should be completed immediately, if not sooner. I knew now that I substituted projects and activities for the time I needed to take to understand myself. I was afraid of being bored because then I would need to think about who I was. I had been avoiding knowing myself well enough to know what to heal.

Nancy added a cautionary note. "We are each guided to do what is right for our own selves. We don't need to put our energy into judgment, even if we feel someone else is doing something the wrong way. We need to concentrate on ourselves and let each person be their own judge of what is right for them. People need to learn their own lessons."

Learn what I can for me, and let others forge their own way. It's unnecessary to judge one another—for me, this was a revelation and a relief.

If I could serve as an example, that would be great, but people needed to learn their own lessons on their own timelines. "Responsibility" didn't have to mean "take care of everything for everybody else." It could simply mean being responsible for myself—the act of responding in order to heal myself.

Emotions, Nancy warned, can cloud the issue, because we can't see clearly when we're emotional. "Use the hawk's eye to see the whole picture," she suggested. "Hawks have tremendous vision and can see much farther than humans."

It isn't that emotions are bad—there's nothing wrong with them per se. For example, anger can be constructive, creating energy for us to move out of a bad situation. But it can also be destructive if, for example, we internalize the anger and it eats away at us.

Sadness is another powerful emotion that might seem negative, but is also a way to cleanse, a way to let go of things. Part of grieving is releasing with love, cleansing ourselves of all we need to relinquish. And too much sadness may lead to depression. It's always a balance. These and other emotions can help us through situations, but they can also cause turmoil. The turmoil makes it difficult for us to make decisions for ourselves. That's where the idea of being centered is helpful.

Being centered is like being in the eye of the storm. By learning how to be the calm within the emotional chaos, we become centered. When we are calm and centered, our vision clears.

It's not necessarily easy. Even Nancy, with many years of experience, admitted that she can't always do it alone. When she can't get centered, she says out loud, "I need help." She has always received the messages she needs when she asks for help—sometimes through somebody else, sometimes from apparently random actions. For example, she picks up a book or turns on the television and sees exactly what she needs to see at that time.

"Then I think, 'OK, I got the message. That's it!'" she said. "No one else sees the message around me, but I know the message is for me because I asked for help. It's all energy. If we do not ask, we will not be able to receive. That's what opening the door is all about."

Musing about Astre and our daily meditations, I noted to Nancy that Astre means "star," and it seemed to me that she was taking me to the stars.

Nancy smiled. "Animals help us heal. They give unconditional love and also help with lessons we need to learn. Astre is a gift that came to help you reconnect with who you really want to be."

It was surprising to think of Astre as a gift. I had bought her because I wanted to compete (yet another example of refusing to relax, despite my best intentions!). But because she was injured, I did not trot, canter, or jump her for six weeks. I just sat on her saddle, my legs wrapped comfortably around her girth as we walked through the woods, which is what we still do. Ninety minutes of relaxed riding through the forest, five to six times a week, with multiple pauses during each ride to meditate.

"Astre the star is helping you get in touch with your unique inner star," Nancy said. "You know what's right for you, and Astre helps you connect with that knowledge."

"Nancy, when I went on my journey two weeks ago in the session with you, were you there?"

"Yes."

"You could see me?"

"I could feel your energy and see other things that were happening. I rarely say anything because my perception isn't necessarily the same as yours. For example, you saw stars; I saw light. When you saw a presence, I felt the energy."

Nancy gestured to the array of crystals that lined the table. "The energy work we're going to do today is directly related to all this.

"The reason a lot of people do not trust or believe in themselves is because their heart is shut down, which shuts down their wisdom. The heart chakra is a really wise area. When people get back to their heart center, it does not mean just emotions. The heart center is where our wisdom is.

"Energy is connected to your heart. Some people can't feel a thing because they are not in tune with their energy, and they use sight for everything. Often people who are shut down completely in their heart area also shut down the sensing of energy. Instead of opening themselves up to the energy, they are blocked in the heart chakra."

I smiled. "The heart is where joy, love, and peace come from!"

"Yes. We house knowledge within us, like computers do. Doubt may appear, but when we apply thought to the energy we flow with, our knowledge, that combination creates wisdom. Each one of us creates our own wisdom, our own truth."

Nancy picked up a crystal. "I talked with your guides, who helped me select crystals specifically for you to learn about."

I was momentarily distracted—how did she talk with my guides? Was this something I could learn, too?—but then Nancy placed an amethyst crystal in my left hand and said, "Your left side is your receiving side. We'll go through each crystal one at a time, and with each one, I want you to notice what you feel. You can learn how to feel the crystal and also sense color. It takes practice, just like anything else."

I gazed at the gorgeous lavender stone as Nancy described its spiritual properties.

"Amethyst is used to calm energy flow. With amethyst,

there could be some addictive thoughts or old patterns that need to be released, which we will work on today."

The amethyst crystal was filled with ridges of dark, softly colored, boxlike formations. I had seen similar stones in Provincetown and artsy stores but had never paid much attention. I didn't notice any strong feelings aside from an appreciation for its incredible beauty.

Nancy cradled another crystal. "Rose quartz, the symbol of love."

I remembered David's and Edward's crystals from the hospital, the quick pulse I felt from Edward's crystal, the minimal response from David's.

I clasped the pale pink crystal in my hands like a prayer book. It was about two inches long and smooth as glass. I visualized my heart chakra opening up to receive, and I felt love emanating from the crystal.

My hands warmed. I thought about love: the satisfaction, joy, and wonder of love. I was surrounded by the energy of love. I sent love to Nancy, Jeff, Ken, and Ryan. I sent love to David and felt myself releasing mountains of sorrow. I sent love to Mom and Dad, to Pam and Jiffy and their families. I sent love to my aunt and uncle, my cousins, my extended family and friends, my companions at work.

Waves of love circled me and encompassed all my loved ones in a warm, safe, and comforting cocoon. Love empowered me. I shared love freely and received love back, multiplied exponentially. I was filled with a deep satisfaction, and I smiled, realizing this was a sign that I was finally learning to love my family and friends first, instead of work.

I gently put the rose quartz back on the table and opened my hand for the next crystal, purple fluorite.

"It helps you connect with your psychic abilities and trust your inner vision," Nancy said.

I squeezed the smooth purple stone gently, enamored with the idea of expanding my psychic skills. I felt the energy of fluorite travel through all the chakras in my body. *Was this energy flow really happening to me, or was I just imagining it?* I glanced at Nancy, who appeared to be engrossed in the dozens of crystals sparkling in her sunroom. She believed in crystalline energy, and I believed in her—and I did feel a difference in my body's energy. I decided that I didn't care if the sensation of energy flow was "just" my imagination; it felt good. And, I had to admit, it sure would be exciting to broaden my psychic abilities.

Nancy held up a stunning bright blue crystal speckled with sparks of gold. "Lapis lazuli has very powerful energy. It helps you express truth. It's been called the Midnight Sky because of its deep blue color and the pyrite, or fool's gold, in it. The ancient Egyptians used lapis a lot, and Native Americans still do.

"The color blue represents the power of communication. Blue symbolizes both the sending and receiving of communication. You might have noticed that speakers wear a lot of blue. Blue is also very soothing. Lapis lazuli is a very deep, emotional crystal."

As I balanced the lapis in the center of my palm, I felt drawn into the crystal's dark blue center, cheered by flecks of golden light. I have always liked the color blue and quickly decided to wear more blue clothes to improve my communication skills.

Next up was the green crystal with red specks. As I held it, I was amazed to realize that the sadness I'd carried with me since I found out about David's illness was ebbing away—not gone, but certainly reduced.

Nancy nodded. "Bloodstone is helping you heal your deep hurts."

Holding the bloodstone, I realized that it was hard to remain stuck in sorrow with all these novel experiences occurring in my life, even though it was David's passage—something I would never have wished for—that had opened me up to these new adventures.

Now I was learning about different realms of existence and different ways to talk with David. There was nothing special about me that caused this epiphany. I truly feel that anyone can access these timeless realms—we need only believe that they are real and allow ourselves to be open to their presence.

Nancy's next explanation—"Feldspar helps people who overintellectualize"—knocked me out of my somber contemplation of death and new dimensions. I laughed so hard that my eyes started to water, and I began to hiccup. I had to admit it: I always tried to out-think and out-maneuver every aspect of my life. I could certainly use the powers of this delightfully striated rock. Nancy's feldspar was light green, but she said it also came in pink or brownish colors. It looked almost translucent.

"You need to be more heart-centered, Becky."

I giggled but said I would certainly try.

"Carnelian came up again to help balance your energies and assist your creativity."

I remembered carnelian, a gorgeous dark rust-orange, from my last session with Nancy. I mentally reviewed my recent behavior. In the three weeks since meeting her, I had been working more creatively, effectively, and efficiently. I was enjoying spending more time with Jeff, Ken, and Ryan instead of working constantly. I was actually having more fun than I ever had before. I needed to keep carnelian around to help me stay balanced and creative.

Next was quartz, which would help me receive Earth's energy and become more connected to it.

The shiny white crystal felt warm and comfortable in my hands. Its visage shimmered with sunlight captured by its sparkling angles. I peered through the crystal and looked beyond.

"A crystal that has a flat side is considered a receiving crystal. It receives energy," Nancy said.

The quartz crystal's flat edge rested on my palm. I felt little tingles of energy being exchanged between this receiving quartz crystal and myself, similar to the feeling I had had with Edward's crystal. But this time, I didn't think I was imagining the feeling. I knew it was real.

Nancy cradled another crystal, celestite. "Sometimes it's called celestine. It helps you connect and stay connected with the higher, more involved celestial energies. It intermingles with the body's own energy and helps us achieve energy flow, movement, and clarification."

It reminded me of amethyst, with all its purple nooks and angular crannies, but celestite was pale blue. I shook my head in amazement at the tremendous diversity of crystals.

"Apophyllite will help with astral traveling." I laughed with excitement and quickly reached for the clear, light-green pyramid of crystal clusters. Astral traveling sounded like great fun. I thought about my journey to the stars where I met God. *Maybe I had already done some astral traveling?*

"Obsidian, also called Apache tear, is here again to help keep you grounded." Nancy gently held the two jagged black crystals and rolled them mindfully between her fingers.

I need more obsidian.

"Crystals all have spirits, you know. Theirs are in tune with nature's energy—the properties of the ones that come from the earth are different from the synthetic stones department stores sell. It does not matter if the stone is polished as long as it's natural."

Nancy traded the obsidian for a large, clear stone about three inches long and two inches wide. It couldn't possibly be what I thought it was.

"Is that a real diamond?"

"It's a Herkimer diamond. Most of them come from Herkimer County, New York. It's actually a special kind of quartz crystal. I use it with clients who don't know what makes them special. They can tap into Herkimer diamond energy, which helps them find their own uniqueness."

Nancy motioned to the massage table, and I lay down on my back with a large smile on my face. I had traveled through Herkimer, New York, when I was completing an occupational therapy internship at Utica College of Syracuse University years ago. It was amazing to think this crystal came from a town I had visited.

Nancy covered me with the same Native American blanket and placed the chosen crystals on each of my chakras. Pachelbel's *Canon in D,* with background sounds of the ocean[29], played quietly. I closed my eyes and took three deep breaths, relaxing my body and mind. In a strong voice, Nancy asked both her guides and mine for assistance during this journey. I felt her hands on the top of my head as she began checking the energy levels of my chakras.

"Your crown chakra is really good, very fruitful, although the energy seems a little low. You are still in self-doubt and continuing some old patterns. I'm going to concentrate on sending energy to your crown to help keep this area open and focused for you."

We were both quiet for a while, then Nancy said, "It's interesting what I'm getting. That little spirit that you saw coming out of the rock…"

"Yes?" I almost sat up, half-expecting that he'd be in the room with us.

"He was so mischievous, he wanted you to see him."

"No kidding?"

"Yes, definitely. His presence was a gift, a gift of love, because you got so connected with the rock. Nature spirits don't show themselves to everyone. They become very happy when a human takes time to connect with them, and that's what you did. He was a funny little guy."

"Yes, he was! I laugh each time I think of him."

"You're going to see more of him. He is going to pop up in different situations. When you work with these spirits, you will experience their great sense of humor."

"When I was in the woods with Astre last week, I saw a fat, three-foot-tall fairy looking at me from the tree line. Was it the same being?"

"No, that was kin of the first being. The energy was different; it was more serious. The fairy you saw in the rock was mischievous and funny."

Now that was interesting. I had apparently seen two fairies on two separate occasions. I hoped I would keep seeing them.

"Becky, I see a light, almost like a star twinkling. I am asking what this is about. I am receiving a message that this is your light. You do not see the light that you are—you see just a little bit. I am sending more energy, and now it's a steady light instead of flickering. Your light appeared small, but it is really very large."

Nancy gently placed her palms on each side of my throat and said, "Your throat chakra is very open." I was glad to hear that. I did express myself verbally most of the time when I had something to share.

I felt the warmth from Nancy's hands as she moved them slowly down my body from one chakra to the next, feeling the energy in each one.

"Your solar plexus is strong and tells me that you overintellectualize. Just relax. Remember the feldspar? Go with your heart. You can learn to trust more in your heart chakra."

Feldspar, chakras, and an underused heart center: I needed to stop intellectualizing and learn to send and receive more love. But how could I do that?

Nancy's confident voice was quiet. "Every time we journey, every time we see something within by using our third eye, there is a message for us. The message does not have to be dramatic. Do not shrug it off. Dreams can also give us messages."

"How do I understand the message without intellectualizing?"

"Feel it in your heart. Now that your heart is opening up, it will speak to you more."

Nancy quickly brushed her hand over my chakras to verify that they were still full, then guided me into my next journey. First I took three cleansing breaths, filling my lungs as full as I could, holding my breath for a count of three, then exhaling slowly through my mouth until my lungs were as empty as I could make them.

After the breaths, Nancy told me to use my third eye to go to my "favorite place"—the place that gave me peace and where I felt safe. She coached me so I could fully immerse myself in this place, feeling all the textures, seeing all the sights, hearing the sounds, noticing the smells, even how it tastes.

When I was settled, she began a guided imagery. "As you stay in your safe place, you see the earth slowly open up for you. There is nothing to fear. The earth is starting your walk with you. Feel the earth's energy beneath your feet. Touch the sides of the earth as you walk inside. As you walk deeper into the ground, you hear the heartbeat at the very core of the earth, connecting with your heart. Follow the beat. Be one with the earth.

"Notice the different energies. Sense the spirit energies, the different colors. They are here. Enjoy them. The earth is joyful because as you heal, she will start to heal. As she heals, you will also heal.

"When you reach the center of the earth, tell me what you see."

I was completely immersed in my journey and described the scene out loud. "Lots of rocks... all different... thousands of crystals lit up. There is no dirt. It is warm and bright... pleasant, peaceful, comfortable. No walls. It feels alive and vibrant. It feels right. Shiny crystals are all around me, and I am in the center. There is a lot of light and water."

I had a very strong feeling that the water needed to be here.

"What do you see in the water?"

"Fish, dolphins, whales, plankton, seaweed, maybe manatees, which could be just because I want them to be here."

"That's fine."

"Sharks, swordfish." I paused, then said, "The water was here first." I felt sure of that, and when I thought about the creation of the earth, it made sense.

"Stars, moons, planets, clouds, and the sky—the whole thing seems like one. It's all connected. And... the creation starts."

"Where are you now?"

"Just floating around. There is a lot of energy, a light in the sky someplace. There are all these worlds. There are tons of worlds!"

"Those are different dimensions. It's great you can see all this."

"I'm sort of dizzy. I don't understand why. I'm just floating, not really moving or traveling."

"You *are* traveling. Just watch."

I sighed; it was so peaceful. Everything was happening at the same time—all these different worlds, different dimensions, different planes, different vibrations—they went on and on. There was no end. There were no limitations.

And I realized with a surprising sense of rapture that I finally, truly understood: There were no limitations in life. There were no limits.

Nancy quietly urged me to reconnect to the crystals that

I saw in the center of the earth. I sent my energy to them and was immediately surrounded by their light. She directed my attention to a huge boulder on my left and asked if I saw the animal behind it.

Was this my spirit animal? Would it be a soaring eagle? Or perhaps a graceful deer, like the one I'd experienced in the woods with Astre? Or maybe a dragonfly, energetic and beautiful?

I could see the boulder and strained to see beyond it, but nothing was there. "The animal is waiting for you," Nancy reassured me. "It does not want to scare you. It has information for you. It's one of the spirits and is going to lead you on a journey. Ask it to come out and show itself."

Something moved, slowly emerging from behind the boulder. It was the most curious thing—about one-and-a-half feet tall, pink and white, almost like a rabbit.

"What color are its eyes?" Nancy asked.

"Blue."

"Good, it wants to communicate with you. Look into its eyes, and it will tell you a message."

"Nancy, I need some help with this one. At first I thought it was a rabbit, but now I don't know."

"Tell me what you see."

"I'm not sure."

"Does it still have blue eyes?"

"No, now it has brown eyes, and a cute little pug nose that's twitching—and it has whiskers. It is definitely not a rabbit. It's lying down... its face is round, with puffy cheeks, and it's brown... now I can see it clearly, but I'm still not sure what it is."

"What does it look like?"

"It might be a raccoon, but it doesn't have the mask. Badger... is it a badger? Damn, I should be able to get this."

"Don't work so hard, Becky," Nancy's voice soothed. "That actually makes it more difficult. Relax, breathe out, and we'll let it go. Just be in the space again... breathe... look at the crystals."

I did as she asked, noticing a wide variety. Most were white, but pink, sparkles of blue, green, glitters of red, and purple were scattered in as well.

Following Nancy's suggestion, I walked around them, touching them, feeling their energies and colors. I discovered I could feel differences. Shifting from a pink one to red felt electric. Red was fiery; blue was calming and purposeful. Purple felt deep.

I could see my animal clearly now, and I knew it was a badger. I had no idea why I was seeing a badger. I don't know if I'd even seen a badger in real life. The badger was staring directly at me, and he certainly looked like he wanted to communicate. Nancy said it was all good and to relay any message I received from him.

I have to admit that I was not pleased to see a badger. I thought I'd see something beautiful and majestic. A badger did not fit my idea of an inspirational spirit guide. I wasn't even sure what a badger was.

Not that it made a difference to the badger.

He spoke clearly in my mind. His voice was strong and purposeful.

"Well, what took you so long?"

I laughed, knowing that I didn't have control over who was best suited to be my guide. The universe knew better than I did what I needed.

The badger said, *Mother, feel connected to the earth, the ground, the sky, the burrows. The earth is pulsing, the earth you helped create. Learn about me. Relax. Rest.*

I listened, trying to stay relaxed, thinking of the oneness of everything, trying to let go and "go with the flow."

Nancy spoke gently. "Keep these feelings in your heart

and start to come back. See the burrow, the crystals. Know you have the ability to feel your own energies... the differences with energy. You are part of this whole universe. You are a co-creator. You helped to create this universe. It's all the divine plan.

"Come back. See the earth, the oneness. Tell the earth you feel grateful for being here.

"Come back peacefully. Know who you are. Know that the more you open the doors, the more knowledge and enlightenment will come to you. Come back."

I took a deep breath, slowly rubbed my face, and opened my eyes. I smiled and sat up on the massage table.

Nancy removed a paperback book from under the table and said, "I have information on badgers for you." She showed me a copy of *Animal-Speak* by Ted Andrews[30], a classic animal interpretation encyclopedia, and opened it to a black-and-white drawing. I nodded my head in recognition: The illustration of the badger looked just like the animal I had seen in my journey.

Nancy summarized the book's description of the badger's significance: "Badger has come into your life. You are quick to express your feelings, and you do not care what the consequences are. Badger people often take on a lot, are aggressive healers, and have courage. They persevere and do not give up. They are tenacious. Badger is often the boss, the one who gets the job accomplished. The badger's certainty is a source of strength."

That certainly sounded like an accurate description of me. I didn't see what the problem was—but Nancy did.

"Badger may be telling you that you have been working too hard."

"No way, did the book really say that?"

"Badger himself told you to relax and rest—and to learn about him. Badger medicine encourages you to begin a new way of thinking about your life."

I pondered that, attempting to process the meaning of the badger. Badger people are "aggressive healers," but was I supposed to heal myself or others? My incredibly strong work ethic rarely allowed me time to consider healing myself. It still seemed selfish and like an unworthy goal.

"You are meant to heal yourself," Nancy insisted.

"So I heal myself and then help heal others?" I persisted, still trying to justify my need to heal everyone else but me.

"Yes, but be careful of your enthusiasm. Remember your friend who backed away after hearing your animated stories? Some people need to be spoon-fed. Giving them the whole dish is overwhelming.

"The message from your badger is that you have the aggressiveness and courage to move forward. It's time to find the pieces of the puzzle and put them in place so you can see the whole picture."

I struggled to understand. Perhaps, as Nancy said, journeying was a natural skill, but that didn't tell me how to do the work I was apparently supposed to do.

"There are many dimensions to this earth," Nancy explained. "Different time periods, similar to different grids in the universe. We can tap into the different dimensions because we are living, multidimensional beings. If you want to travel into the future, you go into a different grid. If you experience a past life, you are in a lower dimension because you would not be as advanced in that lifetime as you are here.

"Everything goes back to love. Love generates concentrated energy."

What a marvelous concept! All people believe in the power of love. Love is the healer, and if love is at the center of the universe, everyone wins.

I thought back to David's transformation into a manatee—another animal I had known almost nothing about—

which reminded me that he had transformed into a raven soon after, pecking on the skylight in Loreen's bathroom to make sure she was OK. I looked up raven in Nancy's copy of *Animal-Speak*. According to Andrews, the raven represented shape-shifting often seen in death, mystery, and creation. It's mind-boggling to think that we have the ability to transform ourselves immediately upon our passage from this lifetime.

David definitely seemed to have mastered this shape-shifting skill.

I left Nancy's home with a warm glow of heart-centered love and happiness. I had always been afraid of being bored, but that day I realized I would never be bored again. There was way too much to learn, explore, and experience in this multitude of worlds.

✳ *Illumination* ✳

Explore crystal stores (sometimes called rock and gem stores), metaphysical stores, or new-age stores that carry crystals. Allow your instincts and intuition to guide you, and pay attention to which crystals attract you.

Place your palm on or slightly above each crystal that draws you. Take a few deep breaths, maybe close your eyes, and see if you can feel the different types of energy coming from each stone. Pick up the crystal and feel its unique energy.

If you like, purchase crystals that attract you. The size of the crystal doesn't matter, only that you are drawn to it.

At home, carry your crystals in your pocket or place them in a special location. Talk with them and handle them—I think of it as cuddling—often. Listen, and be open to what you receive. Consciously choose to believe that you can feel the energy and glean information.

Enjoy learning from your crystals on a daily basis. Explore their meaning by asking them what message they have for you and by reading about their spiritual aspects in books or crystal guides[31-33]. Pay attention to any messages you receive. Above all, have fun.

Shamanic practitioners can teach you how to journey. You'll learn to find your own guides, including crystal, animal, or spirit guides. Once you gain skill, you can journey anytime. The information you gain is incredible. It is all designed to help you achieve greater familiarity and comfort with yourself and the world in which we live.

Always make sure you feel comfortable with your teacher, whether human or spiritual. Trust yourself to make the best judgment for *you*.

I am particularly familiar with classes from the Foundation for Shamanic Studies[34] and Tom Cowan's Celtic Shamanism series[35]. The Society for Shamanic Practice[36] is also a terrific resource. All these shamanic groups have numerous continuing education opportunities and access to shamanic practitioners. Explore the information in the Resources section of this book. If any of it sounds interesting, I encourage you to consider deepening your explorations.

Allow yourself to experience the magic of our universe!

✳ *Chapter 6* ✳

Explorations (EARLY MARCH)

There is no way to happiness. Happiness is the way.

—THICH NHAT HANH

Jeff was carefully loading the dishwasher, meticulously placing each bowl in its proper place. It was Saturday, and the day was wide open.

"Let's go to Bey's Rock Shop[37]," I suggested enthusiastically.

"Sure—sounds like a plan."

"Thanks, dear," I said, giving him a quick kiss. "I really appreciate your supporting me in this. Life would be tough if you thought I was losing my mind."

Ken scrambled into his favorite "Dallas Man" blue winter jacket, and Ryan bundled into his competing red San Francisco 49ers coat. We piled into the Suburban and drove forty minutes north to Bey's. The sign out front was rustic and understated.

As I opened the shop door, crystalline waves buffeted me. My arm hair rose.

"Come on, Mom, let's go!"

I could barely move.

Massive amounts of energy swirled and engulfed me.

I took a deep breath and slowly released it. My body eased out of its stupor. I grasped each side of the door, tentatively placed one foot in front of the other, and moved slowly forward. I blended into the energy field and movement became easier. My body tingled with an ancient feeling of recognition. My face opened up into a wide grin, and joyful laughter bubbled up. There were thousands of crystals here, and their energy was profound. Reds, purples, blues, and golds—we were immersed in a kaleidoscope of color.

I placed my open palm over crystals that attracted me and picked up dozens for inspection. The ones that emitted the strongest energy, I saved. We each had a container to fill. I had no idea where Jeff, Ken, and Ryan were because there were so many rooms overflowing with crystals. No signs explained their spiritual significance, which I guessed helped to keep costs down—most people were here to buy "rocks." I was here to purchase "crystals": rocks with spiritual energy.

I was particularly drawn to the intricate violet amethyst covered with dozens of sharp peaks. The purple hues fluctuated from pale to deep lavender, especially in the center of this high-energy crystal. I carefully placed it in my bucket.

Eventually, we reconvened at the cash register. Between Jeff, the kids, and me, we purchased dozens of rock crystals. On the drive home, we discussed where to put them. When we arrived, we each headed to our rooms and placed them in special locations. I put most of my crystals on my bedside night table but kept a few in my pants pockets.

In the days that followed, I reached into my pockets

frequently, wrapping my fingers around each crystal while squeezing gently. The crystal's energy, warmed by my body, inspired me to send love to David, Mom and Dad, my family, sisters and friends. It seemed like my love amplified when I grasped specific crystals. But then I wondered if it was just a fabrication of my mind.

The bedside crystals caused my dreams to be vivid, colorful, and more real than ever. My alarm clock started emitting unusual chirps, and the radio blared intermittently. I suspected that the crystalline energy was disrupting the electrical current, so I moved the crystals from the top of the clock radio and placed them directly on the wooden nightstand. I felt them sigh in relief to not be engulfed in electrical waves.

I enjoyed talking to the crystals telepathically and quietly listening for a response. Then I felt ridiculous. *What am I doing? Do I really believe that crystals will talk with me?*

I picked up my favorite quartz crystal, closed my eyes, took a deep breath, and felt tingling in my palm. *Did I feel pulsing, or is my imagination working overtime?* The crystal's energy warmed my hand, spread up my arm, moved across my shoulders, and entered my heart. Security, calmness, and peace washed through me. I relaxed until my doubts surfaced again.

One night I thrashed in bed, unable to sleep while thinking about the juxtaposition of my life: conservative business owner and entrepreneur versus new-age metaphysical crystal speaker, fairy believer, and spirit talker. *What is going on? Am I nuts? Maybe I am going psychotic?* I rolled onto my stomach, then tried lying on my back. Nothing worked. Finally I decided to request my guides' assistance. I asked for understanding and fell asleep holding a rose quartz crystal, the sign of love, in each hand. When I awoke refreshed and calm, I chuckled to myself. *Well, if I am going crazy, it sure feels good!*

✻ ✻ ✻

I thought about David constantly, especially since his birthday was coming up soon, March 6. I wondered if I'd imagined all the spiritual interactions that had occurred in the five months since his passage. I tried to forget by drowning myself in work while still looking forward to Wednesday afternoon and my weekly session with Nancy.

"The journey is the most exciting part, not the end result," she declared.

I paused. Goal achievement has always been my prime directive, not the journey. I constantly create new goals so that I can feel good when I succeed. Yet once I reach my goal, I'm left with an empty feeling. I'd never thought about making the journey my top priority. Would that make a difference?

Nancy and I talked about spiritual dimensions, and we discussed time. Nancy assured me that the earth is the only place that has *time*. The concept of *without time* was perplexing. How could there be no time?

I lived my life around time: time to work, time to be with the kids, time to be with Jeff, time to eat, time to sleep. I counted time in minutes and sometimes seconds. It took me seventeen minutes to drive to work... not fifteen minutes and not twenty minutes, but seventeen.

On Earth, we are ruled by time: past, present, and future are fundamental concepts. Nancy said that in space, we light-travel and there is no time. When I journey during meditation, it feels as if I've traveled for days when only a handful of minutes have passed. Which perception is correct? Is time real, or is it a man-made construct that provides boundaries for our earthbound experience, reinforcing the concept that we have only a certain amount of time to live before we die?

Eliminating time means there is no past or future: Everything happens simultaneously. Life is all one. If there is no time and we all live in the present, death will not occur because it implies a past action, and there is no past.

But how can that be?

The experience is the most important part. The journey.

If there is no time, and everything happens "now," our perception of the past is erroneous. All suppressed feelings, emotions, and experiences would be erased if we just lived in the present. No wars would exist based on hidden agendas. No hurt feelings would be caused by prior experiences.

If we lived only in the present, there would be no need for goals because goals require time to achieve. I was startled to realize that my goal-driven philosophy was actually a limitation on myself and my beliefs. When I accepted that time ruled my life, it restricted what I could accomplish and left me empty. I could hardly imagine how free it must be to live without time.

Perceptions are paramount to our reality. Changing our perception of the past can change the present, which in turn will change the future. The present is the most important place we can be. I realized that I don't have to think about the future or always be forging ahead with self-imposed, time-delimited goals. I could, as Nancy said, enjoy the journey.

This conversation about time resonated deeply in my soul, even though I could hardly grasp the concept. I felt my awareness awakening, as if I were remembering information I knew long ago.

Nancy shifted topics suddenly.

"Let's talk about numbers."

Numbers? What do numbers have to do with anything? I was still trying to digest the concept of a world with no time, and now we were going to talk about numbers?

She spoke animatedly about numerology, the meaning of numbers. Many of our ancestors, including the Mayans, felt that numbers were sacred. Nancy believed that if we pay attention to numbers, it can help our understanding of life. She counted off the meanings.

"Number 1 means new beginnings."

This made sense: One is first, something begins.

"Number 2 denotes partnership."

This made sense, too: a duality, a team, companionship.

"The number 3 reflects body, mind, and spirit. It also means when you get everything connected, you can have fun."

Interesting that Christian religious symbolism also includes the number three: Father, Son, and Holy Ghost. I resonated better with the "body, mind, and spirit" concept. And I definitely liked to have fun!

"Four symbolizes foundation, because four corners are needed for a solid one."

A house has four sides, four corners, and a solid base; foundation seemed relevant.

"Five suggests abundance."

A lot of everything: Only four cornerstones are required to build a traditional house, so five was one more than was needed.

"Number 6 describes family."

I grew up with six people in my family. I wasn't sure why six described family to those who study numerology, but that personal connection made the underlying meaning relevant and helped me understand and remember.

"Number 7 is an ancient number that means spirituality, magic, going into different dimensions."

For some reason, I have always liked the number seven. Its meaning definitely seemed relevant to my recent spiritual experiences.

"Number 8 embodies creation and power. This number is often seen on the backs of spiders. Spiders represent creation— they create beautiful webs. No matter how many times you brush a web out of the way, the spider will continue creating its beautiful web of life."

I nodded in agreement, thinking about how the number eight's two circles join to create one continuous, powerful shape.

"The number 9 signifies completion. The circle on top means culmination; the stem, the line under the circle, represents grounding."

Like human pregnancy, I mused to myself. Those were certainly a long nine months.

"Number 0 represents infinity, God: a circle going round and round, with no beginning and no end... infinity."

Infinity. David was teaching me the meaning of infinity.

"Then back to number 1, new beginnings."

I never thought about numbers having meaning, but now I recalled the date David had passed.

October 1... 10; 1.

Number one represented new beginnings—a new life for David. Zero represented infinity—David's life continued, as I kept being shown. Another number one reinforced the concept of new beginnings... a new beginning for myself.

The significance of numbers did seem relevant, at least in terms of David's passage date. Numerology felt a bit far out there to me, but it was worth considering as I tried to figure out the meaning of life and death.

With thoughts of time and numerology churning through me, I asked Nancy, "Do you know what my purpose in life is?"

She smiled as if she had been expecting this question. "I do not know your truths. I could tell you all kinds of feelings I have about you, but they are just my perceptions.

"Your purpose is to find out what is right for you. We each have free will. You can choose to lead your life in whatever direction you desire. Concentrate on the feelings you want to experience, and you will manifest more of the same."

Free will: Are we in charge of our lives, or is life in charge of us? I'd always tried to direct my life and take advantage of opportunities. Yet I didn't understand the significance of life.

Why are we here? What is our purpose? What am I supposed to learn?

I had always filled my life with activity so I didn't have to think about myself. I moved rapidly from one interest to another, exploring, enjoying, mastering a process, then replacing it with something else—and always struggling with the realization that I had no idea who I was or why I was living on Earth.

I'd been rushing through life, finding meaning in nothing. I kept searching for the hidden gem, the kernel of wisdom that would allow me to relax.

David's passage had shaken me to the core, turned my life inside-out, and caused me to rethink my values and behaviors. His continual presence in my life, even after I had thought him gone forever, had opened my eyes to the infinite possibilities of eternal life. I was now learning how connected all life was to everything, and to notice the synchronicities that appeared when we were aware. Even something as basic as numbers can have meaning if we pay attention.

I sat up straight as Nancy began again. "I want to tell you a story about something. It's called the hundredth monkey effect[38]. Have you ever heard of it?"

I shook my head slowly and leaned forward, interested to learn another new concept, although I already felt my mind exploding with so many new thoughts.

"From what I understand, this is a true story. There was an island where thousands of monkeys dwelled. Research scientists visited this site to observe how the monkeys lived and survived. While they watched, one monkey would do something out of the ordinary. Then another monkey would duplicate it, then a third, to the point where all the monkeys on the island were doing the same thing.

"The scientists decided to eat with the monkeys and be friendly with them. They picked up pieces of fruit, washed them, then ate them. The monkeys imitated this behavior and started to wash and eat the fruit. Other monkeys did the same thing until they got to the hundredth monkey. At that point, the scientists noticed that every monkey on the island, no matter where it was, had picked up the same behavior.

"There was another island that couldn't be seen from the first island. Scientists discovered that monkeys living on the second island had also started washing fruit before eating it.

"I truly believe that mass consciousness will take over. As more and more people become enlightened all over the world, others will start feeling the same."

An enlightened world certainly seemed tantalizing.

Nancy placed a print of the yin and yang symbol on the table between us, running a fingertip across its pattern as she continued.

"There are two types of energy. We have a female side— the *yin*—and the male side—the *yang*.

"The black side of the circle represents yin, the female energy, and symbolizes going within—our intuition and introspection. Dreams, messages, the moon, dark, and nighttime— all these are feminine components.

"The masculine side, the white side, is yang, the male energy, representing the sun, light, intellectual clarity, and drive.

"The yin and the yang, the male and the female, need each other to exist. God exists with Goddess. Female energy exists with male energy. Women are as powerful as men.

"Whenever you have a question, ask your guides, your guidance. If the answer resonates well with you, then accept it. If the answer does not feel right, do not give your power away by agreeing with it." Nancy looked straight into my eyes. She seemed to stare directly into my soul as she said, "Believe what you choose to believe."

She rose from her comfy chair and strode to the massage table, motioning me over.

I lay down on the table and closed my eyes, letting her advice swirl through me. She covered me with her Native American blanket and spoke softly and clearly. "We are going to the mountaintop. Imagine yourself dressed as a Native American, riding your horse up the mountain. Face the summit and feel the sun. Feel the warmth. Be aware of the breeze. Look at your clothes. See the colors and the feathers. Slowly climb the peak. Look at the evergreen trees and the foliage. You are ascending higher and higher. Visualize the earth around you. Experience the currents and the energy as you ascend. Your guides are waiting. Look at the beauty of the valley below as you climb the mountain."

I was entranced by the rugged scene as I rode my black-and-white spotted palomino nimbly up the side of this peak.

Nancy's soft voice pulled me further along the trail. "You have reached a plateau, right before you get to the top. A place to keep your horse; a safe spot. You have come here many times. It's a site where you feel connected to the Earth and the Great Spirit. Sense the energy. This is the location of your ancestors who came before you. Return to this area. Feel comfortable, protected, and safe here. Most of all, feel peaceful. This is an area of love, connection, and oneness.

"There is someone who wants to connect with you. Tell me, what do you see?"

I spoke out loud, describing my vision. I had transformed into a muscular Native American male, age twenty-three.

"I am in a familiar place, relaxed from riding my horse up the mountain. The sun is warm, and the sky is peaceful and calm. I look around and wait. I see a shape in the distance."

"Describe the shape. Tell me who wants to talk with you."

"I see a lot of light, lots of energy. It has a painted face." The form became clearer and more focused. "It's an elderly Native American. He is wearing a ceremonial robe and has a huge headdress with feathers off to the side and on top."

I felt safe in this place of power, in the presence of this sacred medicine man. I asked him, "What is life?"

He stared serenely at me, and I heard his message in my thoughts. *You have all the tools to answer this question yourself.*

Oh, brother. It would be so much easier if someone would just tell me the answer instead of letting me figure it out! I took a deep breath, and the words tumbled from me as I tried to describe to Nancy the incredible feeling of peace and power emanating from my guide.

Take care of the earth. The earth is dying. The earth has come full circle and needs to revive. Teach. Learn. Help the earth. Travel within. Be kind. Love yourself. Love one another. Love the animals. Experience the oneness. Teach the message. The earth will be saved. Go within. Come here often. Travel alone. Connect with nature. Show others. Respect the earth and the trees. Bind them together. Send their essence forth like the sparks the Creator sent to us. Be at peace.

I was captivated by this experience. My eyes remained closed. I was fully immersed in this mountainside scene, listening to my teacher.

"Does your messenger have a name?" Nancy asked.

"It's almost like Sh... Shan... Shannee... Son Shannee," I said, my voice filled with reverence and respect.

"It sounds like an Indian name. Is there a translation in English?"

"River... River of Love. River of Peace." I felt a powerful throb from the earth, a sense of affirmation and clarity.

My answer felt correct, and I told Nancy, "I hear the beat of Mother Earth and seem to be floating amongst the clouds."

"Just allow yourself to feel free." Her voice was soothing, nonjudgmental.

I floated, surrounded by peace. I soared with an eagle and saw miles of forested earth punctuated by glorious clouds in a sky so blue, it ached. Far below, tiny specks of animal life bounded endlessly in and out of the valley. I overflowed with gratitude and love.

Nancy felt a different energy appear and said, "Come back to the plateau, Becky. There is someone else who wants to speak with you."

My moccasined feet landed steadily on the highlands. I looked around. An eight-foot-tall brown grizzly bear beamed at me with luminous golden eyes.

"*Co-oome to me and I'll showww youuu the way,*" she growled, her deep roar reverberating through my very being. "*Lo-oooope. Lope as youuu spe-eeeed along the unnn-knownnn pathhh. The lessss traveled way. Traaavellll with-hh-in.*" The words rumbled through me with a powerful ferocity, yet I felt safe and relaxed.

"*Sssit onnnn my backkkk and let yourself goooo,*" thundered the bear. "*Commmme seeeee my familyyyy, myyyy cubs, and beeee withhhhh ussss. Proooo-tect the young and prooootect the earthhh. Leeead the wayyy. Shhhhow the wayyyy and canterrr the trailssss with ussss. Goooo to the spiiiiralssss, the cennntersss. Cooome to creaaaationnn as you expeeerience the onenesssss. Reee-laxxx.*"

We traveled to her cave and cavorted with her cubs. We loped the winding hidden trails together. Peace infused me and reached inside to the very core of my soul. I was connected to all in a profound way, thrilled to be alive in this multidimensional existence.

Nancy's voice, calm and firm, called me back. "It's time," she said. "See your horse waiting patiently for you. Start to return from the mountain, from your sacred spot. Take your time. Come back to this room."

I breathed deeply and thanked the mother grizzly and Son Shannee for their presence and messages. I sent heartfelt gratitude to the universe for all its love, guidance, protection, and wisdom. I felt my soul return to my body.

One, two, three very deep, slow breaths, and I found myself centered and grounded, back on this earth. I gradually opened my eyes and reached up, giving Nancy a heartfelt hug.

"How are you doing?"

"I'm doing great," I said, beaming. "That was excellent!"

Nancy smiled at my enthusiasm. "Traveling alone does not mean you have to live your life alone. It just means going within to get messages from your sacred place."

As I swung my legs around to sit up, Nancy continued. "Energy connects on Earth in spiritual places called vortexes. The earth has chakras, which the vortexes represent. You were told about these sites on your journey—spirals, centers, and more. You can be an earth weaver, Becky, an individual who connects and weaves energies from the vortexes to make them stronger and send them forth. When an area is very congested, it does not have the same pure energy found in nature. Being able to bring energy into a place that needs it is a wonderful gift to present to Mother Earth and her inhabitants."

I was stunned by the beauty and simplicity of these concepts. To be an earth weaver sounded amazingly satisfying.

"You heard the Native American drum, Becky. It gives me goose bumps! You actually felt the heartbeat of the earth, this living, creative being we call Mother Earth."

Nancy reached under the table gracefully and retrieved Jamie Sams' and David Carson's *Medicine Cards*. She flipped through the beautifully illustrated animal card deck, pulled out the card about bears, and summarized the information.

"From the cave of Bear, you find the pathway to the Dream Lodge and the other levels of imagination or consciousness. In choosing Bear, the power of knowing has invited you to enter the silence and become acquainted with the Dream Lodge so that your goals may become concrete realities. This is the strength of Bear."[39]

Nancy lifted her hand to tuck a strand of long, wavy hair behind her ear. "Bears are signs of the north and often symbolize goals and introspection. The bear hibernates in a cave until spring, when new life is born. The bear brought you into her cave, which can represent introspection, going within, and waiting for spring." She slid the card back into the deck and said, "You must go within to find out what is there before you can be reborn."

Nancy turned her head and stared at the rocky hill outside her windows. I followed her gaze to the multihued boulders scattered over a stone mound rising higher than her home. "Life is filled with balancing," she explained. "For years, you have been sending your energy outward. There is nothing wrong with that, but the balance for you is learning how to travel within.

"With one positive, loving thought, you could eliminate a million negative notions. You light one candle in a dark room, and all of a sudden the room is not dark anymore. That is the idea of becoming enlightened. A thousand candles in a room leave no room for darkness anywhere."

I savored this concept of light. Light *is* more powerful than dark. Love, the most powerful light of all, engulfed me in a magical maelstrom of pure positive energy.

Go within, said the bear. *Go within*, said Son Shannee. I needed to travel inside myself, learn who I was, spend time with myself—so I could share my light with the world.

Once more I drove home in silence. I never used to like the quiet, and now it was often my preferred state. I had reflected more in the past two months of shamanic exploration than in my entire forty-two years of life beforehand. It felt great to begin realizing who I was by traveling inward, journeying to different realities, listening, and starting to understand.

Back home, I opened the door with a wide grin, and the kids shrieked their hellos. Jeff laughed and said, "It sure looks like you had fun today!" We gave each other high fives and joyful hugs.

I was so delighted by my day that I was practically babbling. "Jeff, it was incredible! I met an Indian named Son Shannee, and…"

"You mean the Indian tribe? There's one named something like Shannee."

My eyes opened wide. "You're kidding!"

We quickly looked up Native American tribal names, and there it was: the Shawnee Tribe, prominent in the West, particularly Oklahoma. I did not recall ever having heard about Shawnee Indians until that day's journey.

My mind whirled with questions. How did I even know the name Shannee, which I now realized was spelled Shawnee? What did my journeys really tap into, a past life or a long forgotten memory? Maybe I was *not* crazy, if my Native American guide was from a real tribe.

The discovery that the name Shawnee was authentic validated that my journey was based in some kind of reality—didn't it? I was speechless.

Jeff took all this in stride and reacted to my questions by giving me a gigantic hug. He actually seemed impressed that the Shawnee Tribe was verifiable. Ken and Ryan thought my amazement was hilarious. They surrounded me with hoots and hollers and pushed me down to the family room carpet to wrestle.

My joy knew no bounds. I was giddy with happiness. I was living a dream but was wide awake, enjoying every minute of this incredibly profound experience. I couldn't wait to learn more!

❊ *Illumination* ❊

Think about living a life with no time. What does this mean to you? How would you change the way you live if time were not an issue? Would you prioritize differently? Consider what you would modify, and ask yourself if you are ready to change now. A world without time takes a while to assimilate—it took me three years to grasp fully.

Contemplate the possibilities of numerology. Consider numbers that have significance for you—an important date, for example. Do any meanings revealed through numerology provide insight for you?

Ponder the answers as you journey through this lifetime.

✳ *Chapter 7* ✳

Discovery (LATE MARCH)

Human beings are made of body, mind and spirit.
Of these, spirit is primary,
for it connects us to the source of everything,
the eternal field of consciousness.
—DEEPAK CHOPRA, M.D.

I sat at the dining room table transcribing the recording of my latest session with Nancy. My desire to learn was unlimited, and I tackled this new project with the same intensity that I gave to work.

Yet my focus was different. This time I was learning about me, delving inside myself to learn what made me tick. I was not engaging in meaningless activity to hide a profound lack of clarity about myself. I was exploring how to go within to get answers, rather than seeking external gratification from accomplishments or activities. I was discovering how to tap into different dimensions and communicate with spiritual entities.

Shamanic journeying had brought me into a whole new reality. I relished the way it made me feel. I was learning to be peaceful. Profound gratitude flowed from the center of my heart. Love surrounded me.

I asked questions, and answers appeared. It felt like they came from inside my brain, but how could that be? I had never been able to receive solutions like this before.

I must have been learning from my spirit guides. They appeared to have intimate knowledge of my dreams and desires and seemed to want the best for me. Shamanic journeying had opened me up to the presence of these guides, but it didn't insist that I take advantage of the opportunity. If I did not request aid, my guides did not interfere. When I asked my guides to help, they did. If their answer did not feel right, I disregarded it, because nothing required me to accept their opinion.

I had never felt so connected to life or to myself.

I didn't have to succumb to the strong winds of fate blowing me in haphazard directions. I was the master of my own destiny. I felt inner strength that I never knew existed.

A huge sigh of relief came from my soul.

The next day, I woke up singing, "The greatest love of all / is happening to me. I found the greatest love of all / inside of me."[40] Music from this gorgeous tune popularized by Whitney Houston resonated with me. I was filled to the brim with love.

As I stared out the window, a big white fluffy cloud shone below the tree line in the back of our house. I asked for a message and received: *The spiritual realm is here now.*

A huge smile spread across my face. Our everyday world was much more complex and interconnected than I ever imagined.

✳ ✳ ✳

I described my feelings and experiences to Nancy at our next session.

Nancy sipped her tea and stared at me intently, her gaze never wavering. "It all starts with you, with loving yourself. As you connect with people, you will teach them to love themselves more, to love the peace within themselves. You may lose friends or acquaintances who are unable to handle this type of energy. It all begins with you."

As she talked, I pictured love's energy spiraling out into an ever widening circle that expanded each time I was with an acquaintance.

✳ ✳ ✳

A few days later, I had lunch with two colleagues, Caryn Johnson and Kathy Swenson Miller, after giving a guest lecture on marketing occupational therapy. We discussed our recent adventures. I shared my awareness about life's connectedness and how I was learning to find satisfaction within myself. I mentioned meditation and shamanic journeying. Kathy asked if I was referring to religion.

I rubbed my chin and looked away. Were my spiritual experiences religious? I hadn't considered my journey as a theological epiphany, despite my religious background.

I have contemplated religion a lot and wondered if my refusal to attend church came from an overabundance of Episcopalian and Methodist liturgy as a kid. Being a PK, a Preacher's Kid, was a struggle. My siblings and I were always expected to do what was right. I'll never forget when my friends and I wanted to try smoking cigarettes in sixth grade. They quickly pushed me out of the circle just because I was a PK.

Eventually, I stopped going to church because the religious rituals did not make sense to me; they held no meaning.

Nature was—and had been for a long time—a more spiritual domain for me than church.

I believe there is a loving and caring supreme being. I believe in the goodness of all people. After a lifetime quest to discover the meaning of existence, I was starting to understand. Finally, after all these years of searching, I believed in God.

I wanted to answer Kathy honestly, but I was still in the early stages of discovering who I was and what I believed. I had experienced something so vital to my life, so mind-boggling, that I wanted to shout out my discoveries to the world, but I was terrified of the implications. How much should I share? I had probably disclosed too much already.

I was scared that my reputation would be sullied and my business would suffer if I talked about my recent experiences. I was frightened to bare my soul with my esteemed colleagues, concerned they would think I had lost my mind. I looked back at them and spoke slowly, my heart pounding.

"I feel spiritual, not religious. Even though I have seen God, it was more a spiritual awakening than a religious experience."

Caryn looked at me with shining eyes while Kathy nodded her head encouragingly. I quickly looked away, wondering if I had crossed the line.

Sweat beaded on my brow, even though it was the middle of winter. Surreptitiously, I reached into my pocket and caressed four small rose quartz crystals. I felt calmer grasping them and sent love to Caryn and Kathy while trying to slow my heart's staccato beats of fear.

But Caryn and Kathy expressed support, not disdain or disapproval. I took a shaky breath and thanked them for listening. We gave each other hugs before parting.

I traipsed past hundreds of people rushing along the streets of Philadelphia and headed to my car on the third floor of a crowded six-story garage. I felt a little off-balance emotionally; I wasn't steady enough to drive. Energy from thousands of Philadelphians in the area bombarded me. By the time I reached my car, I was ready to shut down. I needed something to soothe my mind as I tried to refocus on reality. *Maybe it's a good time to cleanse my crystals.* I wanted the crystals to remain pure and open to my energy, not teeming with unfocused power from a jillion people. Plus perhaps it would help me settle.

I recalled Nancy's statement that crystals are cleansed with loving intention, and I took a deep breath and closed my eyes. I visualized a powerful white light that beamed down from the sky—it penetrated my crystals and eliminated superfluous energy. I sent out gratitude: *Thank you, universe, for the cleansing power of love.*

Now that the crystals were cleared, I wondered about my chakras. I moved my hand over each chakra and felt the energy. My crown and third eye chakras were strong, indicating a good connection to the spiritual universe. My throat energy was a bit weak, probably due to my questions about sharing spiritual activities with my colleagues. I sent more energy into this chakra, delighted to feel it become stronger.

Nancy explained that she used Reiki[41] to access universal life energy when she checked my chakras. I instantly decided to become certified in Reiki and to keep my eyes open for training opportunities. I wanted to keep learning how to increase my spiritual energy and receptivity.

I turned the key and drove out of the city, contemplating Nancy's lessons: We are spiritual beings confined in human bodies. We have unlimited access to the universe if we only take advantage of the opportunity. We have limitations inside us—yet they can be surmounted *if* we allow ourselves to believe in a life of infinite abundance.

* * *

I tried meditating inside my home but was distracted. Meditating was definitely easier when I was outside in natural settings, especially when riding through the woods with Astre. Nancy had reassured me that as we begin to feel better about ourselves, it's easier to meditate. I still questioned everything, but I was beginning to gain more knowledge about myself, feel more peaceful, and grow more confident in my explorations and experiences.

For the most part, the freedom of meditating outdoors was fine. But one morning, I began to think about creating little nooks of privacy to help me meditate closer to home. I imagined huge trees spread around our yard, highlighted by sunflowers in the front yard and big, juicy blueberries on the side, a big rock or two… what lovely thoughts. Being outside meditating with Astre was sublime, but I wanted to extend my calm demeanor throughout the day. I was always so busy at work, then tried my best to be involved with the kids and Jeff at home, which left little time for me.

One morning, Ryan said he was not feeling well. I offered to stay home with him—and for the first time, I actually enjoyed taking care of my son rather than being mad about missing work. I wondered: Is this the first hint that my drive to succeed is starting to be moderated by myself, rather than by a need for external work accomplishments?

The weekend arrived, and I realized my sense of calmness and inner peace had lasted eight straight days! Could it continue? My parents were coming to visit that night—it was their last stop on the way home after a Florida vacation. I wanted to share with them the spiritual transformation I'd been undergoing, but I had no idea how to do that. The night before, David had visited in my dreams and promised that he would be around to help. I smiled and responded telepathically, *Thank you, David!*

As a kid, I had watched Mom switch roles in the insurance industry when she was repositioned from secretarial work to regional management, showing me how you could reinvent yourself when new opportunities presented themselves. Dad taught me the value of following one's passion when he left the parish ministry and opened up his own private practice in primal therapy and marriage and family counseling. Would they recognize in me similar changes, similar passions? Would they believe and encourage me? Or would they think I was totally nuts?

That night, I looked at Mom and Dad in delight. They were tan, relaxed, and happy to be together with their Pennsylvania family again. The four adults lounged in the family room while Ken and Ryan played with toys on the floor. Mom said she had just finished reading the *New York Times* bestseller *Embraced by the Light*, by Betty Edie[42]. This book describes Betty's experiences of dying, traveling through a tunnel, meeting her creator, then coming back to Earth to continue her life with newfound awareness. Mom was fascinated by these concepts, and her discussion about the book proved to be my perfect entrée.

Jeff sat beside me, providing loving, quiet support as I began my story slowly, feeling my way. Birds chirped greetings from our secluded backyard. David was present but did not dominate my energy.

I shared that I had found inner peace and calmness. Both Mom and Dad raised their eyebrows at this—"calm" had never been a word anyone would use to describe me before now. Yet I did feel serene, a remarkable achievement in itself.

I brought out the huge three-ring binder that housed my word-for-word session transcriptions with Nancy. Dad read through the first meeting. "Why does Nancy interpret symbols for you?" he asked, with a shake of his head. His question didn't come from disagreeing with her interpretations, I knew. He just preferred that people figure out their own issues.

"Nancy doesn't force her spiritual interpretations on me, but they do help me understand," I explained. "She always asks if her statements resonate with me. If they don't, I just disregard them or come up my own interpretations."

"How does that work?" Mom asked.

"She communicates with her own spirit guides throughout the day. She says we must always ask permission to speak with someone else's guides, and I gave her that permission during our first session. Since then, she has spoken with my guides in the mornings of days when I have an appointment.

"It's made such a difference—I feel changed for the better inside myself and in the way I interact with people! I am finally gaining a tiny inkling of who I am and what my purpose is on Earth. I love what I'm learning."

I rested my journal on my lap, tracing its cover with my fingers, noting my nails bitten down from stress. From spirit guides to—I took a deep breath and continued.

"I travel to different realms of existence during meditation. It's called shamanic journeying, and I meet all types of spirit beings."

I opened my journal to the drawing of the fairy. "About a month ago, in the early morning on the first day of our corporate retreat, I spent several hours by a lake."

I handed the journal to Dad, who studied the sketch briefly before passing the journal to Mom. I told the story of what happened that day, culminating in the flash of green shooting out of the stone and the sketch that appeared when I tried to write about the experience.

Mom stared and said, "You saw this?"

"I don't remember seeing it, but I drew it when I wrote about the green flash that came out of the rock just as the sun peeked over the lake." I shrugged. "My mind couldn't process seeing a fairy, but it registered it, and not long after, I drew it.

You should have seen me try to lead the corporate retreat while my brain kept switching to the fact that fairies must be real. Despite that, or maybe because of it, the retreat was incredibly successful. What was even more amazing to me was that the next time I saw Nancy, she said fairies were all over me, and I hadn't even told her I'd met a fairy!"

Mom and Dad glanced quickly at each other, then at the sketch, then at me. I'm sure my face was glowing with excitement.

"Come on, Grandma and Pop-Pop," Ken blurted out. He'd heard this story more than once; it was time for something new.

Mom said, "That is an amazing story, Becky." Dad raised his eyebrows but remained silent.

"We want to show you our rocks!" Ryan proclaimed, tugging on his grandma's hand.

"Yeah, c'mon, Pop-Pop," Ken urged.

I laughed as they trooped upstairs, thrilled that my parents hadn't lambasted me for being crazy.

Gales of laughter and oohs and ahs echoed from the boys' rooms. I was delighted thinking of all the crystal energy flowing through our home.

Jeff lit the dinner candles as I spooned food into our china serving dishes. I love using these dishes—crystal and china from Jeff's family, accented by special pieces from Mom and Dad, Grandma and Granny. Just holding them made me think of how much love was among us.

"Dinner's ready!" I called.

Ken and Ryan whooped with joy as they raced down the steps, shoving each other to see who could reach the bottom step first. Mom shook her head at all the commotion, but Dad took her arm, and they entered the dining room hand in hand. We settled into our places and clinked our glasses in good cheer. Conversation continued long into the night.

David flitted in and out; he remained a significant part

of our family from his own realm of existence. Each time I mentioned that David was around, Mom and Dad looked a bit startled, but told me to share that they loved him and missed him a lot. David heard this message and beamed his love, enveloping us in a cocoon of camaraderie.

I passed David's crystal around the table. Mom and Dad said softly that they had never seen it before but remembered David speaking occasionally about his crystal. They each fondled it lovingly, staring off into space, tears glistening in their eyes. I felt a warm, constant glow when it finally returned to me.

The next day, Mom and Dad left. We promised to visit them soon.

Still feeling the glow of my parents' acceptance, I decided to experiment with crystals. Could I re-create the journeys I had at Nancy's home, but here in my household?

I closed the bedroom door and settled on my back on top of our queen-size bed. Breathing deeply from my solar plexus region, I breathed slowly in, then out, each inhale deeper, each exhale slower. My body relaxed; I felt open and receptive.

I tried to keep my mind clear. When I thought of something mundane, I breathed deeper and relaxed my shoulders, hips, and ankles as I sank into the mattress. I concentrated on my breath. Errant thoughts were whisked away, and I flowed into oblivion.

I sent a questing message telepathically to my guides, consciously opening my mind and listening—and I heard very clear instructions in my head! Immediately I decided to acknowledge what I was hearing as real and listened with rapt attention.

"Place the citrine crystal on your crown chakra," instructed my guide in a deep, clear voice. *"Citrine provides warmth and abundance, and it represents the sun. Unite earthly pleasures with spiritual awareness.*

"Use carnelian on your third eye. The autumn orange color promotes harmony with the earth. Carnelian calms fears about death and rebirth. It is a harvester of dreams and helps you see past lives.

"Position sodalite and rose quartz on your throat chakra. Sodalite enhances rational thinking, facilitates deep thinking and knowledge, and unites logic with spiritual wisdom. Rose quartz is the love stone. It will help you manifest self-love, mother love, nurturance, and forgiveness.

"The heart chakra will benefit from malachite for loyalty. It draws out negative energies, is used for cleansing, and expands inner clarity and self-understanding.

"Place clear quartz on your solar plexus to promote knowledge and communication.

"Your sexual creative chakra does not need a crystal to enhance its qualities.

"Place the Apache tear crystal on your base to assist you with grounding and as a reminder of Native American energies.

"Under your body, position a clear quartz crystal to help show you the way."

My guide's message was seared into my brain, and I had no problem remembering. I had all these crystals, too—I purchased most of them recently. I remained in meditation and, with heartfelt sincerity, telepathically transmitted *Thank you so much* to my guide.

I opened my eyes and gathered my crystals.

I was ready.

I lay down again, visualized a protective white light surrounding me, and placed each crystal on its appropriate chakra. Immediately I felt my chakras expand with power and resonance from the crystals. I closed my eyes and took three deep, cleansing breaths.

My journey began.

Raven, my bird totem, picks me up. We burst into the sky and speed toward planets and stars, passing them in a blur of light. Our rapid, spiraling ascent makes me dizzy; I remember to breathe slowly, deeply, and my dizziness dissipates.

We reach a place with dozens of bright luminescent green energy spots. I quickly meld into one of these glowing energy centers. The energy pulses with knowledge. I have become one with all creation. I am rapidly shown how to use my hands, the palms of my hands, and then my whole body as a healing tool to send positive, loving energy into people or situations. I am inundated with love and compassion. Joy radiates through my mind, body, and soul. I am transformed into a beacon of light.

Love emanates from this remarkable green energy. Love emanates from me. Love is sent to the whole universe on multitudinous waves of light. I bask in the glorious power of love.

The scene changes.

At first I think it's a path, but no, it's a road. Animals are standing alongside the road as if waiting. Those nearest me include a polar bear, an elephant, a snake, and a fox. I ask for a message.

"*Use your instructors. Trust yourself. Travel within. Learn the messages of these guides. Become familiar with their essence.*"

My head bows respectfully as I greet the polar bear, elephant, snake, and fox. My heart feels open and overflows with love.

The raven beckons. It's time to go home. We wing back through multitudes of dimensions and land on familiar ground. I thank him from the very center of my heart. He blinks his bright yellow eyes in acknowledgement and flies off.

I slowly opened my eyes, gathered the crystals, and reached for my pen to record this grand adventure. I basked in the comfort of knowing that I could now journey and meditate at home, as well as in the woods when riding Astre.

Discovery (late march)

※ ※ ※

Each day, I became calmer. Work remained exciting and interesting, but now I had other things in life to consider. My family, my inner spiritual growth, Astre, and all my guides were becoming increasingly important.

Work had always dominated my life. Everyone knew my priorities, including my kids. I always said "Work comes first" when I had to explain my inability to attend a sporting or musical event. I never felt guilty about this philosophy, for I sincerely believed my intense work ethic helped me succeed in the business world.

But now I was starting to realize there was more to life than work. My family was relishing our increased time together, and we started to plan more family experiences.

During this time, the journal where I recorded dreams and spiritual experiences rapidly expanded. One night, I had a vivid dream about David and asked where he was now. I got the distinct impression that he did not remain in one place but traveled around. I asked if he had seen God and he said, *"As a matter of fact, no! And I am really pissed off. But I do have this ancient scroll that tells me what I am supposed to do."*

My alarm clock pealed its noisy clatter, and I was unable to return to the dream. I laughed out loud thinking about David and his ancient scroll. I called Loreen, and we giggled as I told her my dream. We both knew that he always hated to be told how to behave—he'd work ten times harder his own way rather than follow directions about what he *should* do. For him to be stuck with an ancient scroll that told him what to do definitely proved that the universe had a sense of humor!

While riding Astre not long after my dream about David and the scroll, I encountered a Native American female spirit guide who was extremely assertive and demanding. She wanted to teach me about herbs, healing, and using my powers. She demanded, "*I have waited a long time and want to teach you now!*"

I tried to listen and learn because I enjoy these subjects, but she quickly became aggressive. She started to block messages that I normally receive from trees, rocks, and other guides. Her energy did not feel good. I realized she needed to be sent away.

I remembered my lessons and understood that we only need to accept spirit guides who come to us in love, filled with warmth. We all have free will. Each of us has the power to control what we want to see during meditation. We can always open our eyes to clear our mind of the images during journeying.

I visualized a large white toilet bowl. I imagined this spirit guide being flushed down the toilet in a whirlpool. I watched her spin round and round until she disappeared. I thanked her for trying to teach me but explained that her demanding methods were not helpful.

After I flushed this overbearing spirit down the toilet, I looked up to the sky and saw her overhead as a large wash of light. She already appeared less powerful.

I was pleased with how easily I had sent away this guide, but I wondered why she came to me at all—normally I had peaceful, thought-provoking meditative journeys. Two days later, I meditated and quietly asked to see this same woman again to ask why. I received a surprising answer.

"*This guide represents an aspect of you—your aggressive behavior that at times attempts to force views on others.*"

I felt like I'd been caught red-handed. This statement was more true than I would ever have admitted on my own. The "rightness" of it astounded me. And, just like flushing the aggressive form of the guide away, I realized I had to commit to no longer being so domineering with my viewpoints. Humbled, I thanked the guide for clarifying this important message.

It is amazing how journeying meditation works. The information I received from my disgruntled guide, just by asking lovingly for her to return, was presented to me with love. I could deal with the implications of her message because the message resonated so well with my increased self-awareness. I said again, "Thank you, spirit guide, for your clarity, wisdom, and love."

The next day, I meditated and sent Nancy love. Later that day she called to say, "Thank you, Becky, for your prayers!" I glowed as my face burst into a wide smile. The love you send can definitely be felt!

Three months earlier, I had gently placed David's crystal on my home office windowsill where the sun could reach it daily. Nancy taught me that crystals could be cleansed by intention and also by placing them in the sun. The first time I had seen David's thin, five-inch-long quartz crystal was in the hospital on the night I met the manatee. Then it was heavy, gray, and dense. Now it glistened and sparkled with pure white luminescent rays. I reverently brought it up to my heart and beamed, "I love you, David." The crystal emitted a warm pulse, and my heart sang.

A few days later, I received the name of an unknown crystal during my daily meditation. The crystal's name sounded like "chal-ca-done." I could not get this word out of my head, so I wrote it down on a yellow sticky note and stuck it on my dashboard next to other notes reminding me of various important things.

I puzzled over "chal-ca-done" throughout the day as I drove to visit clients and provide customer support to our new agencies.

At the end of the afternoon, I noticed a small wooden sign for Brady's Village Art Gallery and Rock Shop[43] on the side of the road in Berks County, Pennsylvania. A large carved eagle sat majestically in the front yard of a large house. I felt drawn to enter.

Hesitantly, I turned the door handle. The first thing I saw when I entered was a large amethyst crystal sitting on top of a tall cabinet to the right of the door. Its sparkling purple radiance emitted beautiful energetic waves, and I immediately felt welcome.

Hundreds of colorful crystals, many in small white labeled boxes, rested on glass cabinets spread through the room. A light layer of dust covered part of the rock artistry in a darkened corner in the back, but most of the space was bright and cheerful. The varieties, colors, and shapes of these crystals were stunning. I breathed deeply and slowly, allowing myself to receive whatever message had brought me here.

I reached for a pale orange crystal and cradled it in my hands, opening myself up to feel its energy. I read its accompanying label, nicely typed with a short sentence describing its country of origin as Argentina.

Captivated by the quality and variety of this extensive collection, I strolled around the room, drawn by the pull of the crystalline forces. There were tiny one-inch bright-green stones from Africa, a beautiful sky-blue gem from Ethiopia. I lifted up four gray geodes, about two pounds each, that Ken, Ryan, Jeff, and I could crack open ourselves with a hammer to discover sparkling minerals inside.

It would be great to learn how to prospect for crystals. I would love to be guided by the energies of the world, explore caverns and fissures, and find stones of spiritual magnificence. *Someday, I'll learn*, I promised myself.

An attractive middle-aged gentleman entered the shop from a side door. He wore a tweed jacket and a jaunty cap and was clearly the owner. He welcomed me with a cheery greeting and began to putter around the store, letting me continue my explorations.

I watched him casually move around his collection of

crystals, straightening up as I gathered a small mountain of spiritually enticing rocks to consider taking home.

Despite my assumption that he was enthusiastic about his collection and wouldn't hesitate to share what he knew—a trait many business owners, including myself, share—I stuttered awkwardly and blushed deep red as I fumbled with the sticky note. Doubt assailed me. Why was I even here? He was going to think I was a total jerk.

"Ah, I was wo... wondering," I stammered, "if you, um, had ever heard of the name chal-ca-done?"

His eyes twinkled and he said, "Why, yes. It's pronounced *kal-se-doh-ne*. Let me show you!"

He reached under the counter and handed me a stunning light-green crystal about four inches long, interspersed with peaks of white. I was stunned. The chalcedony energy felt pure, and I said without hesitation, "I'll buy it!"

I looked at my scribbled note and realized the name I'd received was very close to the correct spelling of this crystal. Once again, I received clear validation that the information I obtained in meditation was credible.

The next week, my dear friend Toni Esposito and I had lunch. We'd met ten years earlier at a medical equipment sales conference, back before I started my business. Toni is an excellent salesperson, and I had always admired her easygoing personality and friendliness.

We'd talked before about my spiritual experiences, but it was still a surprise when she asked me to communicate with her dog Rex, who'd recently passed. This wasn't something I'd tried before, and although I'd known Toni for years, I'd never met her dog. I asked my inner guides if I could do this. After a second, I received a strong *"Yes!"*

I gave Toni a rose quartz crystal to remind her of the shared love in our deep friendship. Then we feasted on a wonderful lunch, reminiscing and catching up. After we finished, we ambled over to a grassy park close to the restaurant. I wanted to be outside for this experience.

We sat down beside each other on a park bench in front of some large oak trees, to the left of a park dumpster. I reached for my own rose quartz crystal.

"Let's each hold our crystals and close our eyes. Uncross your legs—the energy seems to flow better when it can move freely up and down our bodies. Keep your feet flat on the ground and breathe deeply. When you are ready, think of Rex."

We sat quietly, our faces turned toward the warm and comforting sun.

Immediately I saw a dog lying down, wagging his tail. I shared my vision with Toni, and she quickly confirmed the coloring: It was Rex!

Toni was having difficulty visualizing her beloved pet, possibly due to her intense distress at his passage. She posed questions to me, and I sent them to Rex.

Her most important question was why he had died when both she and her husband, Jim, were away.

Rex put his head down between his paws and whimpered. He did not want to hurt Toni or Jim, he explained. He thought it would be easier to pass this way. He also left his body before the pain became too severe.

Rex seemed very happy to be with Toni again. His tail wiggled constantly during the rest of our conversation as he ran peacefully around a white earth-type setting. When I relayed this to Toni, she exclaimed, "He always wagged his tail, no matter what! Please send him all my love."

Suddenly, a small dog came right up to me and sniffed, wagging his tail happily. I quickly opened my eyes to confirm that I was seeing a dog both in my mind and in Earth's physical reality.

Toni asked, "Becky, can you talk with my other dog, Brookie, too? He passed away a number of years ago."

I asked Brookie if he wanted to appear, and then I waited. After a few moments, a small white dog manifested in my mind. I wasn't certain it was Brookie, and I told Toni that white often symbolized spirituality. But Toni was confident that Brookie was present, and she asked me to send her love to him. I described the vision I saw: Rex and Brookie running in circles, playfully nipping at each other's legs, then racing off into the horizon.

Toni and I sat on the bench for a few more minutes, basking in the magical love with Rex and Brookie. We opened our eyes slowly and gave each other a huge hug, feeling peaceful and content. It was only forty-five degrees outside, but we both removed our coats. We were very warm after communicating with her beloved pets.

On the way home, I started to feel slightly disoriented and had the sense of a headache. I reached for the Apache tear crystal in my pocket and held its grounding energy in my hand for the rest of the drive.

Later, when I shared this experience with Nancy, she said that the headache probably came from my quick transitions in and out of meditation. She encouraged me to make sure I was clearly grounded after each spiritual session, which I had not done. I was enjoying the peaceful, otherworldly time with Rex and Brookie, and I had not brought myself back consciously to physical reality. Before driving home, I should have pressed my feet firmly on the dirt and reached down to touch the soil with my palms while visualizing myself back here on Earth.

March had been my most intense month of spiritual adventure and growth to date. Gratitude filled my soul as I wondered what would happen next.

✳ *Illumination* ✳

Try to communicate with a person you love or a pet who has passed on, especially if you have experienced a recent loss. Believe you can do this. Go into meditation using whatever method works best for you. Ask for your loved one to appear. Acknowledge that whatever sign, feeling, word, vision, or image you receive is communication from your loved one *if* it feels right.

The more you accept the possibility that you can communicate with loved ones who live in different dimensions of reality, the more they will communicate with you.

Always send love. Always thank them for sending you love. Heartfelt gratitude definitely assists with this communication process.

Communication with loved ones who have passed on will happen more and more if you trust it can occur. Try not to be too critical of your attempts. Keep trying.

Believe.

Chapter 8 ✳

Guided Communication with Lot and Other Spirits (APRIL–MAY)

When words are both true and kind,
they can change our world.

—GAUTAMA BUDDHA

I've been an occupational therapist since 1976, well respected by my peers. I spent my entire adult life building my business and reputation in this field that I love. I even went so far as to plan the births of my children around our industry's major annual event, the American Occupational Therapy Association Conference—which, to everyone's surprise (including mine), actually worked.

I headed off to the 1996 conference filled with joy and excitement about the transformation I'd been undergoing, practically bursting with stories about my experiences that had begun with David's passing. After receiving support and acceptance from my parents, my husband, and several close friends among my colleagues, it never occurred to me that my enthusiastic pronouncements about having extraordinary spiritual experiences, including seeing fairies, would be met with anything other than curiosity and delight.

I swept into the opening meet-and-greet reception, exuberant and ready to reconnect with colleagues I hadn't seen since last year's event.

The room was filled with people. They balanced drinks and hors d'oeuvres, clustering in groups that formed and reformed as old friends greeted each other and newcomers introduced themselves.

I was barely in the door when a colleague caught sight of me and asked how my year had been.

"I met a fairy!" I exclaimed.

She looked puzzled, as if she hadn't quite heard me—not surprising, considering the din of so many people talking. I raised my voice and said, "I really did connect with a fairy—a fairy! Fairies are real!"

She stared at me for a moment, then turned away and began talking to someone else. I didn't give her reaction a second thought: That's the way these events go, people changing direction, interrupting, shifting to a new person, a different conversation, all the time.

One of the leaders in our field nearly bumped into me. "How's business?" she asked, clearly glad to see me.

"I had the most incredible experience," I gushed. "I met a fairy."

Her face paled, and she stepped away, looking aghast—which only made me more determined. I didn't quite ambush the next colleague I knew—first we talked briefly about a chapter on home health practice I'd written—but when she asked me what I'd been up to. I said, "You won't believe this, but I met a fairy."

She hesitated, then said, "Well... that's good, I guess," and after a brief pause, continued in her best "therapist" voice, "I'm glad you think you saw a fairy."

After that, there was a long, awkward silence. Neither of us knew how to proceed, and I slowly realized that years of "competent" behavior and a successful business in the occupational therapy world were not enough to counterbalance my colleagues' doubts about my sanity. My enthusiastic storytelling wasn't convincing people that fairies were real or that I'd experienced something profound. Instead I was convincing them that the Becky they knew and respected had gone off the deep end and could no longer be trusted.

It took me years to regain my professional credibility— but the conference was not a total loss.

It was the last day of sessions. I made my way through a roomful of round tables and chose a seat beside a Catholic nun. I was entranced by the concept of combining religion with occupational therapy. Perhaps her life story, if she was willing to share it, would provide some insight or direction.

Within moments, we were deep in conversation about spirituality. She described a workshop she had recently attended where a New York psychologist spoke about "automatic writing."

"It's when spirits write messages to us. Our hands move across the page, seemingly on their own," she explained. "When it happens, your pen actually moves without conscious thought, guided by the spirits."

I was fascinated by this concept, of course, intrigued by the possibility of another communication channel with the expanded world I had begun to explore.

I arrived home late Sunday night, excited to see my family. I greeted Jeff with a smooch and tiptoed into the kids' rooms to give them a kiss hello as they slept. I fell into bed, glad to be home and looking forward to my morning horseback ride. On

Monday, I arose as usual at 3 A.M., rushed to work, then left at 7 A.M. to ride Astre. We thoroughly enjoyed ambling through the forest. During our two-hour ride, I meditated about four times.

My meditations were filled with messages about teaching spirituality. It was hard to comprehend instructing others on this subject, especially while running my business—and especially after recognizing the responses of my colleagues at the conference.

But I do love to teach. I realized that I definitely needed to improve my confidence as well as my approach if I were to speak effectively in public about my spiritual adventures.

I groomed Astre and led her to pasture, where she could graze and enjoy the sun. Before heading back to work, I sat in my van and recorded the morning's meditations. I'd been keeping a journal since the beginning, as it helped me remember the messages.

I was in the middle of writing when all of a sudden, my pen started to move across my spiral-bound notebook on its own! I watched my right hand slide effortlessly across the page, writing words that were not coming from me, but which were in my own handwriting.

I watched in shock. What was this? Was it automatic writing? It must have been—and I could either freak out and probably make it stop, or go with the flow and see what happened.

I chose to see what happened.

Two sentences rapidly appeared.

"I will discover power in me, especially in my hands, power on this earth. Learn how to harness its energy and ride it forth to the winds above and the earth below."

The winds above and the earth below? I never think like this.

I barely had enough time to read what I had transcribed as my hand continued to record. *OK, Becky,* I told myself, *just relax and let it flow.*

My cheap black Bic pen scrawled under its own volition, words streaming behind it.

"Investigate the oneness of life, the spirits below and above. Go with the flow. Surround the earth with love and peace, kindness and goodness. Be calm. Be centered. Be watchful. Be respectful. Show yourself. Travel the earth. Have fun. Enjoy life. Good-bye."

"Good-bye?" I squealed. "Who are you?"

My hand moved quickly in response: *"I am love."*

What? I was too stunned to say it out loud, but the question connected and—

"I am Lot."

—wrote itself on the page.

"Why did you come to me?" I asked telepathically.

"I wanted to show you how journaling works."

I wrote "Thank you!" in big letters.

"You are welcome. I love you."

"I love you, too!" My heart blossomed.

"Be at peace with yourself, Rebekah. Love and show others how it is done. We will be watching and waiting. Enjoy."

I had never experienced strong vibrant energy like Lot's before. His message felt similar to those I received during my shamanic journeys, yet the words on the paper made the transmittal more vivid. Stunned, I read and reread Lot's message. I could hardly believe this had happened.

Until yesterday, I'd never heard about automatic writing. Today, I received a beautiful message conveyed by it.

I glanced at my watch and realized I was already late for work, according to my strict, self-imposed schedule. I rushed off, showered quickly, and submerged myself in the daily grind, trying hard to forget about Lot and automatic writing.

But that evening, I relayed my morning adventures to Jeff. He was flabbergasted and wanted to see if I could repeat the process with him present. But I was not confident enough to try it again, especially in front of someone else, even someone I loved and trusted completely. Not yet.

The next morning, I began my day with meditation, and Lot came back!

"Hello, Rebekah. You are joy and happiness. You are you. Be light. Be alive. Do not plan, for it will come. Flow. Go forth and spread our message."

"How would you like me to go forth?" I wrote my question quickly.

"Go forth in love, in peace, in harmony with the world and with nature. You are not alone in this universe. There are others. There are many. Search them out, and then you won't feel so lonely. Talk with Nancy, she is one. Talk with others. They are here.

"Rest now. You have done well."

"Will you come back?"

"Of course I will. You are my vessel, my messenger, and my standard-bearer. I can speak through you."

Once again, I realized I was definitely not making up this conversation. I never use the word "standard-bearer."

The next day, I told Nancy about everything that had happened: meeting the nun who was also an OT, my apparently automatic writing, my connection with Lot. She smiled and said calmly, "The universe is filled with surprises."

I'd been second-guessing myself about this phenomenon, even though all I had to do was look at the writing in my notebook to realize something remarkable had happened. Nancy's acceptance of Lot's presence reassured me and reinforced my belief that what I had experienced was, in fact, automatic writing.

As we talked, I realized my views on death had changed significantly since David's passage six months ago. Ever since I learned to communicate with David in his life in another realm, I had accepted that people do not die, they just "pass on." Rarely did I use the words "die" or "death" anymore. We just change dimensions and continue to grow and learn forever when we pass from this world.

Since his passing, David and I had communicated about once or twice a month. He was usually upbeat, but the last time he'd seemed unhappy. I thought everyone who passed on would be relieved of problems and be happy and content.

"There's an old phrase," Nancy explained, "*Uncle Herman is still Uncle Herman on the other side.* People who pass on and live in another dimension are still the same people they were on Earth. They keep learning."

"I sent David tons of love," I said. "I even called my sister Jiffy and asked her to send him love, too."

Nancy nodded. "That's exactly what you should do. You'll help David by communicating with him and sending him love just as if he were sitting here talking with you."

I leaned forward in my chair, feet flat on the ground, hands clasped between my knees, and looked straight at Nancy. "I finally figured out how to tell people what I'm doing with you without sounding like a complete crackpot!

"Most people are willing to accept that I have seen David and spoken with him since he passed on, because they are familiar with NDEs: near-death experiences. That's a much better conversation starter than saying I saw a fairy jump out of a rock!" I shook my head ruefully, remembering the conference fiasco. "I asked David if it's all right to share our experiences, and he assured me it was fine."

Nancy pointed out, "Intentions are powerful. We have to be careful because ideas are very influential. Thoughts are our creations. We create energy when we think and when we pray."

Nancy always talked about prayer. I liked the word "intention" better, perhaps due to my inner Preacher's Kid still rebelling against the entire concept of prayer. But whether you call it prayer or intention, the action, the hope, is the same.

"When you journey, your intention is always to receive and give the 'highest good,'" Nancy continued. "You can reiterate this request every once in a while to reaffirm the concept, but you do not need to repeat it constantly—and you shouldn't, because that would be like saying you are not trusting. Request your highest good, and you will obtain it."

In other words, ask and ye shall receive. Maybe those long-ago lessons weren't as off-base as my rebellious PK self wanted to believe.

I reached into my briefcase and retrieved my notebook with the handwritten messages from Lot. I caressed the front cover. Reverently, I pulled out a page of transcription I had typed for Nancy because my scribbling was difficult to read, and I passed it to her.

Nancy scanned the page quickly. "This is wonderful! It gives me goose bumps!"

She paused to read it carefully. I sank into the chair, reviewing the scrawled message for the umpteenth time. I still found it hard to believe that Lot was communicating with me this way.

"Becky, you can call these teachings whatever you want, but sometimes labeling limits opportunities. If you function only within the confines of a label, it can stymie further exploration.

"You are re-remembering who you are; I am helping you recollect because I can see your potential. Some might label me a healer, but I think of myself as a facilitator. Learning to accept and recall ancient wisdom uses a variety of techniques including shamanism, spirituality, and understanding oneness within yourself and the universe. My task is to facilitate your explorations using the techniques best suited for you at any given time."

Nancy spread her hands wide, encompassing the world inside and outside her home. "You have allowed yourself to try a variety of approaches without prejudging the consequences—therefore, you receive. You are certainly in the flow, drawing what you need to advance your learning without judgment.

"Judgment is a major complication in life that creates tremendous turmoil." Her right and then left hand opened, palms up to the sky. "What is right? What is wrong? When we analyze a behavior, we make a judgment about it for ourselves, not for others. The teaching may not be right for us, but maybe another person needs it, can learn from the experience and find something they need to understand. We are responsible only for our own world, actions, and awareness."

Grandma, Grandpa, Granny, and Jeff are all teachers. Dad and Gramps are ministers. I'm an occupational therapist. Each of us cares for others, first and foremost. To take care of myself first? That was a philosophy I'd never learned. I'd never known who I was, so how could I take care of myself, even if I knew it was an option? Nancy's teaching—facilitating—combined with my spiritual explorations since David passed were expanding my awareness and educating me about myself, helping me discover who I was. For the first time, I was learning to be responsible for me first.

I felt a great unburdening, as if my soul had sighed in relief.

I gazed at Nancy, sitting comfortably in her overstuffed chair. Her long, sable hair framed a mind filled with wisdom. I felt contentment tinged with anticipation for whatever would come next.

After a quiet moment, Nancy said, "Becky, I've been guided to have you tap into one of my relatives whom you have never met. See what you can receive."

I cocked my head to the side, eyebrows raised in surprise. This request felt different from connecting with spirit guides, and different from the communication I had with David. I took a full, deep breath, closed my eyes, and silently repeated the name Nancy provided.

I felt a distinct energy associated with this name. I telepathically asked permission to continue communication and received a strong *"Yes."* A variety of images and feelings flooded my mind.

After a few moments, my thoughts clarified. I spoke out loud, slowly at first and then with increasing confidence as Nancy verified this person's age and marital status, sex, and number of children. I shared feelings associated with the tableau I visualized in my mind. I was stunned to realize that I could feel energy associated with an unknown individual who was not present in the room. This spiritual communion was incredibly validating, especially when Nancy confirmed my observations. But I questioned the morality of using this ability and vowed to always ask permission to communicate before barging in unannounced.

✳ ✳ ✳

Through my work with Nancy and my own mindful practice, I was becoming more aware of other people's energy, whether I was at work, home, or our kids' activities. I consciously visualized my heart opening, expanding, ready to receive… reaching out without judgment to allow my companion to share honest and open feelings if they desired. I felt a person relax, almost whisper, as they innately acknowledged the intimacy of our energy exchange. Some people were closed, and I was unable to sense energy through their defenses. That was OK, too.

But when I did connect with someone on this intimate energetic level, there was a freedom, a sense of peace, and a soaring of emotions that felt magical. Navigating interpersonal dynamics during my workday and at home was transforming my energy awareness, particularly when I spoke from my heart. It felt good to speak with love. People perceived the love that was being offered, and they often responded in like fashion.

I was also learning the benefits of manifestation. Using intention to manifest our highest good helps create our own utopia on Earth. I always used to plow ahead, aware of my own desires but not necessarily alert to how they affected others. Now I perceived the depth, complexity, and importance of our interrelationships.

I discovered that synchronicity occurs when mutual desires connect. Each action causes a spiraling reaction that relates to our past, present, and future. When we ask for our highest good, life's pathways become clearer. We can learn from each experience as we head toward our destiny, living in a community of like-minded souls.

The benefits of these discoveries extended beyond the spiritual. Around this time, I realized my headaches had essentially stopped. I had taken six to eight aspirin almost every workday for ten years. Over the past few months, my aspirin consumption had dropped to only two to four a week. My stress level had considerably receded as I scheduled more time for myself and for my family, without always putting work first.

When I realized my headaches were vanishing, I wondered if there was a way I could help my office friend Carol Harding. Migraines had plagued Carol for as long as I'd known her. I asked if she wanted me to try to relieve her next migraine and explained a little bit about what I was learning regarding energy. She agreed, and a few days later arrived in my office mid-migraine. We shut the door and turned off the lights. Carol sat on a firm wooden chair, her brow furrowed in pain. I stood in front of her, closed my eyes, took a long, deep breath, and focused on my spiritual center. I asked permission from Carol's guides to work with her and received an affirmative answer. I moved slowly toward Carol's head and felt a massive spike of energy, like a spear or a sword, coming from her right temple. I softly asked her where the migraine was, and lo and behold, it was in the same place I felt the energy spear! My skepticism about being able to feel Carol's headache rapidly dissipated.

Gradually I moved backward, following the trajectory of the energy spear, my hands held out in front of me next to each other, palms face down and fingers extended toward each other, gently touching at the tips to create a wide cupped space.

The migraine spike extended eight feet out from Carol's head. It felt like a pulsing core of white and gold energy piercing the air. I stood at the far end of the spear and, very slowly, started to weave my hands back and forth, gently guiding it toward Carol's head while continually asking for her highest good to be achieved. I watched Carol's reactions carefully to make sure my speed and process were comfortable for her.

Her eyes were closed, her face calm. After ten to fifteen minutes of slow, gentle weaving, I reached Carol's head. I gently pressed the last remnants of the spike back inside her temple and sealed it with thoughts of love, returning this transformed energy to her compassionately, rather than shredding it, which I intuitively suspected could cause more suffering. I rested my hands on her temple, sending love and healing into the site of her pain. Carol's body position and facial muscles were relaxed. The tension wrinkles on her forehead were gone. She slowly opened her eyes in wonder.

"How are you feeling?" I asked softly.

"I still have a slight pain in my head, but the sharp, pounding migraine is gone. That felt really good. Thank you!"

My face beamed, and I immediately sent love to Carol's guides, thanking them for their assistance. Carol and I shared a big hug as she left the office, ready to resume her day.

Later, as I reflected over the impact of studying with Nancy since January, I realized that before I had an awareness of energy, my life had seemed dull and bereft of passion. Now I felt totally different. I was more self-aware than before David's passage. I knew who I was. I knew why I was here. Recognizing that energy surrounds us, resides within us, is present in all life forms, and is an integral part of our universe had quickly become natural. I realized life was a continual process, and I did not have to accomplish everything right *now* because I was going to live forever. I had all of eternity to grow and experience the oneness that I now felt in myself and with all of creation. I relished family time and no longer felt as pressured to work all the time. I was finally learning to take time for me. Working with energy had been, and continues to be, amazing.

* * *

Every day, I meditate. I especially love meditating with Astre. We walk through peaceful woods and gaze at the trees, listen to birds, and smile at flowers blossoming under the forest mantle. Frequently during our ninety-minute ride, I pull up on the reins, take a deep breath, and relax into the saddle to meditate. Astre stops walking, bends her strong neck toward the earth, and meditates with me. We sink into oblivion, and our spirits soar.

One day, I sent my spirit into a big brown hawk circling above us. I luxuriated in the feel of my strong wings stretched on the spiraling winds.

A flutter of blue butterflies gamboled nearby. I thanked my hawk friend and sent my spirit into the center of the kaleidoscope of butterfly wings. My razor-sharp hawk vision and commanding presence were gone, but there was no lessening of spiritual intensity or awareness. In fact, with my smaller butterfly size, my senses were more finely tuned; I noticed and responded to the smallest movement in the air. Our wings flittered joyfully as we glided toward flowers rich in nectar.

A warm breeze rustled my antennae. I found myself drawn to the breeze. *Thank you, butterfly*, I whispered lovingly in my mind. I opened my spirit up to the wind and was immediately swept into a powerful burst of energy. I soared with abandon, releasing all control to the current.

Freedom, a sense of ecstasy, coursed through my soul. I whirled and twirled, tumbled and dove in a surge of power, safe and protected, the wind my chrysalis.

I was drawn to the sky and perceived hundreds of different dimensions and thousands of universes. I realized Earth was just one of the many places we can access through the power of meditation and love. Ancient knowledge filled me, and I knew I was part of the whole, separate yet deeply connected, integral to all.

I was stunned by the simplicity and profound realization that love was the center of all life. Love and gratitude flowed and overflowed inside and outside my body. I smiled from the very core of my soul.

Finally, it was time to return.

I groomed Astre, massaging the spot where my saddle sat on her back, and walked her into the field to graze. As I sat in my Suburban and began to journal the day's meditations, a light, airy presence entered my mind.

"Does someone want to come through?" I wrote.

"Yes, yes, yes! We are the fairies, come to provide you with love, joy, and happiness. We love your reading about us, the angels and the wonders of nature. Have you missed us? We have been there, and here, and everywhere. We love you!"

"Who are you?" I asked, smiling. The joyous energy coming from these beings was infectious.

"The fairies! The fairies! Why do you not believe?"

"So sorry! Forgive me!" I quickly recorded while sending them love with my heart wide open.

"We want to say hello to you!" My pen scratching across the page was the only noise in the car, but I heard each word, too: childlike voices singing in an uplifting chorus of loving harmony.

"Hello to you!
Hello to you!
And now we sing
a song for you!

"We love you, too
We love you so
We will run and play
Along with you!"

Now they serenaded me in a new harmony with high-pitched gaiety. *"Come out and play with us! We want to teach you about love, sex, happiness, freedom, and fun. Pure enjoyment. Glory be to the one on high that we respect and enjoy. We bring laughter into lives. You can, too, with your playful manner and watchful eyes. You can teach. Teach the masses how it is. Have fun. We will be watching and waiting."*

"How can I learn to do this?" I wrote rapidly.

"Play with us. Go outside. Laugh. Live. Experience nature. Enjoy the spiritual wonders and beauty."

"Are there books I should read?" I love to read, especially fantasy and books about real-life spiritual adventures.

"Any you want, but particularly ones by Lynn Andrews [44-51] *and Ted Andrews* [52]. *Ted is a master. He will help you understand our beauty. We want you to understand so you can teach our glories, our glorious personae. Thank you for*

177

believing." I was utterly captivated by this two-way conversation occurring in my mind and in my notebook, and I told them so.

"Our beauties have been hidden for ages, centuries, eons. People have become too rigid, too set in their ways, too grounded. They need to be uplifted. Warmth, love, possessions... but "possess" none, or they will possess you. We travel light. Enlightenment will come your way, and Jeff's, too. We love you, Becky. Thank you for carrying forth our message."

"Thank you for believing in me!" I responded heartily.

"Thank you for caring."

"I love you, fairies! Teach me how to live, and how to do this!" I said, then grinned when I heard tinkling bells and peals of laughter.

"We will! We will! We will!"

I was filled with joy! Fun ways to teach people about the fairies were already streaming through my consciousness.

After a moment of rapture, I glanced down at my message-filled journal, startled. Was I crazy? Did I just talk with fairies? I reread the words. It's one thing to draw a picture of a fairy, but to hear a group of them chattering away was either crazy or incredible.

I did an immediate reality check with myself. I knew my name, the day of the week, and my birthdate. *I'm an occupational therapist. I've been married to Jeff for eleven years. We have two sons, Ken, age eight, and Ryan, age six. I just finished a horseback ride with Astre. I meditate every day.*

I looked around the car. Yes, this was my car; it was solid and real. I was still here, solid and real. How could I have just talked with fairies?

I needed to get back to work.

* * *

178

I spent the next few days immersed in office tasks but did reveal my latest spiritual communication to my family and a few close friends. I tried to temper my desire to share—I still did not want people to think I was nuts, especially when I was questioning my own sanity.

I opened my journal, ready to meditate. Immediately Lot's presence entered my mind. Lot's energy was very different from the fairies'. His felt loving but masculine, focused and direct. Fairy energy was happy-go-lucky, joyful, and free. Lot's message was from him alone. Fairy communication came from a multitude. But both the fairies and Lot used the same communication method: a presence outside myself filled my mind and drove my pen across the page.

"Hello, Rebekah. Lot here. It is interesting to see you progress in the light of the love overseeing all Earth. Carry the beacon of love and peace, joy and happiness. Live pure and free, be kind and good. Be one with the Creator, your Creator. Travel within and without, a circle of love and laughter.

"Have fun with the fairies. They will teach you how to laugh and enjoy life above and beyond the experiences of the now. Learn from them. Watch. Participate. Savor the tremendous energy they inhabit. Live your life with them. Show them and the world the miraculous peace that can ensue.

"Be creative with your goals. Your goal is your goal, not designed by anyone but you. Listen. Learn. Respect. Wonder. Have fun.

"Relish the peace that surrounds you. Enjoy life to the fullest. Be aware of the pitfalls. Do not get carried away by the love of it all.

"Be suspect of those that tell you what to do. Listen to yourself.

"Love. Love yourself, Jeff, the boys, the people, the animals,

the spirits, the spirit guides, the angels, the archangels, the nature spirits, the sprites, the elementals, and the world.

"The world is a wonderful creature, a being, a soul. A beauty to behold. Wait for your time on Earth. It will come. I love you."

"I love you, too, Lot. Thank you so very much. I love your messages."

"I love your messages, too, Rebekah. It's fun to talk with you. You are my vessel for love and messages. Go in peace."

I read Lot's message multiple times. I had never, ever experienced thoughts like this. My head bowed in disbelief.

The next day was Sunday, and I didn't need to work. I got up early, sat at the dining room table, opened my journal, grasped my pen (resisting the urge to bite the top, which I'd already mauled), took three slow, deep breaths, and began my morning meditation. Almost immediately, I received my third message from Lot.

"Hello! Lot here to wish you a happy Mother's Day. Glory be to mothers! Transcend spirituality and transcend motherhood to reach the people beyond all worlds."

All of a sudden, I heard Ken and Ryan call for me.

"Mom, you hear them calling. Go—I'll wait."

I ran up the stairs. Ken, Ryan, and Jeff all had their arms out to give me celebratory hugs and kisses. "Happy Mother's Day," they gushed, handing me presents. We sat on the bed, and I opened gifts. Group hugs and laughter filled our home.

Finally, I returned to the dining table. Sun streamed into the room and cast a golden glow on my journal. I closed my eyes and breathed deeply. I felt Lot's presence immediately.

"You are a good mother."

I grimaced, thinking about all the times I had not been present for my kids due to my overriding need to work.

"Do not negate the power and love inherent in motherhood. Mothering: a skill we all can use and need at some

time in our lives. You are a good mother, not spectacular but certainly good. It is a new role for you. You are growing into it. The past year has seen good growth in your learning about mothering. Love, live, laugh, and enjoy being a mother, Rebekah. I love you."

"I love you, too, Lot! Thank you!"

"You're welcome, Mother."

I ponder Lot's Mother's Day message. My whole life centered on work even in childhood. In high school, I had four jobs at the same time, and I thoroughly enjoyed each one. I'd never had spare time.

Until now, I'd spent time with Jeff and our kids only after I finished work. Or, if I allowed myself to attend one of the kids' school functions during the day, I returned to work as quickly as possible. I got up early in the morning to work. I came home late in the evening after attending multiple meetings. I tried to be home to kiss the kids goodnight a few times a week, but I was not always successful.

Jeff and I married when we were in our early thirties. We were both independent and career-driven before marriage, and marriage didn't change that.

I made a conscious decision to get married specifically to have children. I hoped parenting would help broaden my horizons and give me something new to focus on besides my job. I didn't want to die from overwork. Yet my workaholism became even more pronounced as my company grew beyond all expectations.

Since David passed and I began learning about spirituality, I had found myself enjoying the mothering process more than ever. I appreciated knowing, at least from Lot's perspective, that my parenting skills had started to improve.

I sank back into meditation and was quickly transported away from the hustle and bustle of Mother's Day.

Immediately, I recognized the singsong chorus. The fairies were here!

"Me! Me! Me!"

"Hi, fairies! Great to be with you again!" For some reason, I thought about David.

"We'll help you be with David! Come on, David! Come and play in the woods with us. Call David, Becky. We'll help."

I sent a telepathic message to David, filled with sisterly love and friendship.

David arrived quickly and we laughed exuberantly. David, the fairies, and I danced atop mounds of moss, somersaulted across the grass, and frolicked among the trees. We relaxed in the gaiety of the moment, thrilled to be together again. I sent a heartfelt *thank you* to the fairies for allowing me to spend time with David and them.

David's presence gently ebbed away. I was filled with love. Love for David, love for the fairies and Lot, love for Jeff, Ken, and Ryan. Love for the universe. And—love for me. I was slowly realizing that it was OK to send myself love. I felt a sense of oneness with the universe, a deep gratitude to God and the universe for sharing these lives with me. My mind, body, and soul rejoiced.

My eyes fluttered open. This was an awesome Mother's Day!

Normally I meditated in the morning, but two days later, I decided to try a new time of day. I settled in to meditate in the evening. A different spiritual being entered my mind.

"Hello. Where have you been? I have been waiting for you!"

"I've been here all day. I didn't realize I needed to ask," I sent telepathically.

"Sometimes you do," replied this visitor gruffly.

"Are you Lot? You don't sound like him."

"I am Lot's companion, SoJo. Wisdom comes from

within, from the depths of many. Many faces, many thoughts, many minds. The wise woman knows when to stop, when to rest, when to have peace. You need to rest, Becky. You have been working too hard. Why do you work so hard? What significance does it have for you?"

I paused while my brain processed this question. I liked to work! I relished challenges and appreciated seeing positive results.

"You will see results when you rest," SoJo chided. *"Your mind needs rest. Relaxation cleanses the soul. Relax, Becky, and have peace. We love you. Now go to bed!"*

SoJo's message resonated deeply. Maybe I shouldn't meditate in the evening. I did feel tired, and I did need more sleep! "Thank you, SoJo," I shared telepathically. I took a deep and refreshing breath, opened my eyes, shut off the light, kissed Jeff good-night, and went to bed.

I woke up to rain and decided to ride Astre. But first I worked two hours in my home office, got the kids up and dressed for the day, had breakfast with them and Jeff, then drove them to daycare. It was only 7:30 A.M., and I still had plenty of time.

Astre whinnied a greeting. I curried her coat, luxuriating in her soft, smooth hair. I picked the snow and dirt out of her hooves and telepathically sent heartfelt thanks to her for being such a wonderful horse.

We meandered through the woods. It had become simple to meditate in the forest, with no one around except for hundreds of trees and the chitter-chatter of bird talk.

Rain sprinkling forest leaves like dewdrops of joy splattered the ground in gentle pulsing cycles. My heart opened to the universe. I sent energy into a tree and shared love. My spirit felt alive and free. I completely forgot about work and my life on Earth.

I called for David. He seemed a bit farther away. "Thank

you, David, for helping me access this dimension so that I can communicate with you and other spiritual beings."

David replied grudgingly, *"You are the one that did it, not me."*

I reluctantly agreed that I was the one communicating with spirits, but if it weren't for his passage, this would never have happened. I was sure of it.

"Do you have any messages for the family?"

David nodded his head.

"Tell Jiffy I love her and miss her," he said with great feeling. *"Tell Mom not to try so hard."* He sighed. *"Dad, spread kindness, goodness, and love around. Pam, take care of yourself and your new baby. Loreen, I miss you. Travel your own path, find a companion if you want. Becky, continue to learn, relax, and take more time for you."*

"I love you, David," I said with heartfelt thanks and appreciation. I was excited to share his words with my family.

"Why did you choose to shapeshift into a manatee?" I queried.

"They symbolize the demise and destruction of people with AIDS. I am familiar with the plight of manatees from my sailing trips and don't want the same decimation to happen to them."

I understood. Our souls shone with mutual clarity and love. "Thank you, David, for showing me the way." David faded away.

After I finished my ride, brushed and groomed Astre, and rubbed her long nose good-bye, I sat in my van flipping through my journal. The written messages from Lot had grown longer with each meditation, from a scribbled half-page that first day to six handwritten pages in the most recent session. I relished this written correspondence, but I wondered how much more of it I could take. During our meditations, I would hurriedly shake out my wrist to alleviate the cramping that began after three or four pages of intense, almost frantic, writing. But what else could I do?

On the seventh day of daily visits from Lot, he implored, *"Rebekah, use your computer!"*

"My computer?" The juxtaposition of Lot and current technology seemed beyond weird. Typing on a computer was so modern; Lot's presence felt old. Using my computer to record ancient knowledge felt like a major mismatch.

Lot disagreed. This was simply a new method, which he called "guided communication." Typing would work just as well as my scribbling, he assured me.

Using my computer to transcribe Lot's words still didn't seem right, although it did make sense, sort of. I am an excellent typist, about 90 words per minute. I used to have races with myself when I was a kid to see how fast I could type. I loved the challenge and immediate reward of seeing words typed correctly on a plain piece of paper. As a high school student, I would sit in my attic bedroom typing for hours, racing to better my speed each day. Typing would solve the problem of trying to interpret the poor penmanship that resulted from scribbling quickly to keep up with Lot's communication. I wanted to record every word.

After a moment of contemplation, I disengaged from Lot, rushed downstairs to my home office to retrieve my computer, hurried back to the dining room table and turned it on, my heart beating wildly. I took a deep, calming breath and closed my eyes, my fingers in home position on the keys. Lot came back immediately. I started to type, and voilà: The transcription process immediately became easier. Lot's words flowed from my mind through my hands and onto the keyboard.

I kept my eyes shut, which intensified the meditation connection. I typed without interpretation and was only about 70 percent aware of my surroundings during this process. After I finished meditating and thanked Lot, I read the message and spell-checked it, being careful to portray his words accurately. I reread the corrected message and saved it under his name, Lot, and the date. I have continued this guided communication meditation method ever since.

* * *

I had begun reading Ted Andrews' book *How to Meet and Work with Spirit Guides*[53]. I could still hardly believe I was talking with spirits. Ted described Archangel Michael, and I decided to ask him to appear almost as a test. If I could reach Archangel Michael, it should prove to me that I could communicate spiritually.

I surrounded myself with love while taking three long, deep, slow breaths. I cleared my mind, relaxed my shoulders, arms, and back muscles, and focused deeply on communicating with Archangel Michael. My hands were positioned over my laptop keys. I asked for my highest good to be realized.

Within seconds, a powerful spiritual energy appeared in my mind. He was very confident and communicated clearly with me.

"Hello, Becky. You are learning about me."

His energy was unique, commanding, and intense—masculine and strong, but totally different from Lot's and the fairies' energy.

I was stunned to receive communication from another entity, even though I had asked for Archangel Michael to appear. Without thinking, I let his words flow from my brain into my hands as I began to type.

"Now is the time of all men to come together and be joined in love for all eternity. Love beyond the universe, beyond the boundaries of all men. Help to guide the unsure."

I could hardly believe this was Archangel Michael. I couldn't wait to show Jeff. I knew he'd be stunned.

All of a sudden, the information stopped flowing.

I pondered… and realized that the moment I stopped paying attention to the message, it ceased. OK. I needed to get focused again.

Becky, I said to myself, *relax. Stop thinking. Just absorb.*

I breathed deeply, turned off my brain and left it empty, ready to receive.

The words from Archangel Michael returned. I dutifully recorded.

"I am Archangel Michael, come to you from above planet Earth to show you the way. We have chosen you as our messenger of light. Do not let your ego surface or get in the way. You are one of us. One of all people. Be watchful. Be wakeful. Challenge and learn from yourself. Be true to you. Be happy. Be at peace. I go now."

"Why leave now?" I received the answer instantly. Without hesitation, I transcribed it.

"I gave you my message. Carry it forth."

The authoritative voice stopped. I tried to resume meditation, but no words or images appeared. I felt like an empty vessel, almost drained. I slowly opened my eyes, breathed deeply, and stared out the window.

That night after work, Jeff and I read the message, both shaking our heads in disbelief. We read the words again and again. Lot and Archangel Michael both used words and phrases that I would never think of using myself.

I shared the messages with Ken and Ryan. They weren't as skeptical as I thought they'd be. I guess talking with spirit guides and angels was not that unusual to them—they were young and probably thought this was normal behavior.

We'd always talked about magic in our house. Santa

Claus visited our home every December, regardless of whether the kids believed or not. For a few years, I was a professional entertainer on the weekends, Bubbles the Clown. My children saw me transform into Bubbles and produce all sorts of magic. Maybe they assumed spirit guides and angels were part of the magic that lived in our home.

Jeff and I often spoke with Ken and Ryan about how people have different belief systems. We said that it's totally fine for everyone to think what he or she desires—there was not one right way to process. People have the right to believe what they want in their own fashion. Along those same lines, I did not ask them to believe in the new spiritual communications I was receiving, but I did present the information. They seemed to accept it, and they could see that it made me very happy.

A week earlier, we'd been talking about spirit guides and animal totems. Both sons said they would like to know their totem animals. I got the beautifully illustrated *Medicine Cards* deck[39] Nancy had used, and we all gathered around the worn teak coffee table in our family room. While shuffling the cards, I asked for guidance to assist our sons in choosing animal guides for their highest good. Then I spread out the cards facedown on the table.

Ken reached first. He took a deep breath, and, trusting his intuition because the back of the cards all looked the same, carefully chose nine cards of the forty-four. When he finished, we turned each card over, exclaiming in delight. I wrote down the animal names, then reinserted the cards and shuffled the deck.

When I passed the cards to Ryan, he flashed an impish grin and cut the deck. He plucked his nine divination cards quickly, then leaned forward to discover which animals he had chosen.

Each son had picked entirely different cards. "These animals are your friends. They want to teach you about nature and their own special powers. Just ask them to come," I explained.

Then I read a brief summary of their totems' spiritual meaning from the *Medicine Cards* guidebook, reinterpreting the message to make it relevant for young children.

I laid out their chosen cards again. The boys fingered them, each picking up their special cards and staring, reordering, and placing them in different positions. After a few moments, they'd had enough and raced to the basement to play video games.

The next day, Ken, our second grader, asked to go on a journey. I immediately sent a telepathic message to his guides and asked approval to assist him. Almost simultaneously, I received a very strong confirmation: *"Yes."*

Ken lay down on his back on his bed and closed his eyes. I did some energy work on his body, opening up his chakras to help him receive the information he needed, and said, "Breathe in through your nose and out through your mouth three times." He appeared relaxed, calm, and ready.

To begin guiding Ken on his first shamanic journey, I asked him to travel in his mind to a very safe place where he felt comfortable and protected. After a moment, I asked softly, "Where are you, Ken?"

"With you, Mom."

I beamed, thrilled that I was his "safe place."

"You will meet an animal to guide your journey. It will be very safe. Take your time, and tell me what you see."

Ken spoke in a quiet but normal voice. A deer, one of his totem animals, had greeted him. I understood: The deer represents gentle healing.

Ken and his guide pranced off together. They romped across the land, jumped over logs, and leapt through meadows and fields. Soon they rose above the earth, where fairies, each holding a sparkling light, greeted them. The fairies and Ken frolicked in the sky.

After about ten minutes of describing his journey experiences, Ken murmured that he and the deer were returning to Earth. "Thank you for guiding me," he said reverently to the deer before slowly opening his eyes.

He looked angelic, radiating incredible calmness and peace. I reached down and gave him a huge hug. "Great journey, Kenny! Well done!"

I gave him a glass of water. As he drank deeply, I explained, "Nancy says it's important to drink water after journeying to help cleanse and refresh ourselves."

I handed Ken a small rose quartz crystal as a reminder of his first journey. "Rose quartz is the love stone. You are loved by me, Daddy, the fairies, the deer, and by all the Creator's creatures on earth." Ken wrapped his hands around the rose quartz and brought it to his heart, then carefully placed the crystal on his bureau before scampering off to play with his friends.

I marveled at the ability of an eight-year-old child to sense the oneness of creation and sent thoughts of gratitude to the spirit guides for helping Ken and me experience such wonder.

✳ ✳ ✳

The next day, during meditation, I asked Archangel Michael, "How am I supposed to communicate your message of love and peace?"

"You already know how to do this," he said, his voice filled with the confidence of authority.

I was stunned at the depth of his belief in my abilities. I wished I felt as convinced as he clearly was.

I called Nancy for reassurance and explained that I seemed to be moving pretty fast with all these spiritual experiences. She agreed, and even said she was learning from me!

Well, that was certainly hard to believe. I told her that I

couldn't imagine what knowledge she was acquiring from me. Her answer—that she was discovering how to accept experiences without fear—surprised me at first, but then I understood: I was not afraid of my spiritual adventures because they felt so right. I questioned their validity and certainly my sanity, but I was not afraid.

Nancy reiterated that God's work is love. "We are all one. With God, everything is possible. When fears come up, it's all right to acknowledge them and then overcome them. Life is an experience, so therefore experience it. God does not push. God is love."

Yes: The oneness of life is transformed by God's love for all of us. There is no need for judgment. We are love. God is love. I am love. We can't go wrong with love.

In the twenty years since I began meditating, I have accumulated thousands of pages of guided communication messages from Lot and hundreds of other spiritual entities. From the beginning, Lot encouraged me to share his messages. Soon into the session when I first began using my laptop, I'd also asked him, "How do I spread the message?"

The response came instantly. *"Don't disseminate yet. Gain strength from the many. Be active in the metaphysical community. Relax and enjoy."*

I sighed in relief as I remembered Lot's teachings—I didn't need to publicly share my experiences yet.

I saw myself as a woman with long blond hair and smiling blue eyes, lying on a billowy white cloud, my head pillowed on my arms. Soon I transformed into a beautiful monarch butterfly with fluorescent orange wings and black markings highlighted by twilight blue. My human body was in the middle, the thorax. I felt my wings and antennae pulled up, up, up to the sky past the earth, clouds, and stars… "Hey, wait for me!" I shouted. "I want to come, too!"

My spirit was rising fast, but I was held back by the physicality of my human body. Then—*whoosh*—I became fully immersed in my butterfly persona, beating my wings in joyful harmony with the world.

My wings fluttered in rapid staccato as I dipped and swooped with the winds. I travelled farther than I ever had before, soaring higher and higher until I met God once again.

"My child," he called me. My wings had become transparent, and my pulsing heart emitted streams of light that mixed with God's pure, clear energy. We swirled and whirled in a cascade of love that filled my soul with bliss. We blended together, becoming pure white energy that vibrated faster than hummingbirds' wings. God's love filled me with energy, and my heart shouted with joy. I was entranced.

Slowly the vision dissipated.

I started the return to Earth, moving in a slow descending spiral. I passed the cloud I originally rested upon and sent it love. A sparkling waterfall appeared, flowing into a deep pool of clear water. I dove deep, shivering with the cold but feeling refreshed. I floated on my back and gazed in ecstasy as a rainbow burst over the horizon like an arc of rapture. Reds, oranges, yellows, and greens shimmered and shone as they melded into blue, indigo, and violet. Droplets of sunshine fell lightly from the gleaming arc.

I opened my eyes and took a deep breath. I asked for guidance about my journey, and the following message popped into my head.

"Butterfly means metamorphosis. You are being transformed.

"When you stayed on the ground and your butterfly spirit was trying to ascend, this signified choice. You could either stay grounded or continue your metamorphosis. You chose to proceed with your transformation into a spiritual being.

"God sends you energy, love, peace, and goodness.

"Diving into the sacred pool purifies you. The rainbow signifies happiness and shows you are accessing a number of dimensions by its wide variety of color arcs. The droplets of sun denote a spreading of warmth, love, and peace."

The next day, I rode in the woods with Astre. I was once again becoming overwhelmed by all these spiritual messages. I deeply wanted to learn more, but I continued to doubt the reality of my instruction. How could I be communicating with all these guides? Was I making this up? Why me? What was going on?

It was becoming harder and harder to concentrate on life's daily realities. I asked my guides for specific instructions on how to proceed, then let the question go. I did not dwell on the request. I waited for my answer.

Astre and I rambled through the woods until we reached a familiar spot, the crossroads. Two paths intersecting with no clear indication of which direction to choose, but there seemed to be no wrong way. I released all my earthly concerns and sank into meditation as Astre gently stopped.

A deer and her baby appeared. I immediately shape-shifted into the fawn and nursed from the doe's teat. Three other fawns were present. We rested and drank milk, receiving food and energy from our mother. I wanted to bound away, but Mother kept me with her as I gained strength, security, and self-reliant confidence from her. After a while, I left her protection and leapt away to discover my own path. I relished the freedom of being alone, yet understood that Mother would always be with me.

I opened my eyes slowly and gave heartfelt thanks for this reassuring visualization. Like the fawn, I, too, was gaining the confidence to proceed on my own. I understood that I would be taken care of and provided for during my journey. I gave thanks to the doe, the spirit guides, and the universe for showing me the way.

Astre and I walked deeper into the forest. I spied Jack-in-the-pulpit wildflowers that reminded me of my grandmother, Anne Pifer Austill. I'm Granny's eldest grandchild, and my middle name is Anne. I've always been pleased to be named after her.

Granny loved the natural world and was a connoisseur of flowers. She'd spent many years in Japan mastering ikebana, the Japanese art of flower arranging, which became a lifelong hobby. I marveled at her ability to showcase the beauty of just one or two flowers arranged in a simple curving movement pattern.

For most of my life, Granny lived in Cape Cod, where her wildflower garden was both a playground for holiday adventures and a quiet place of respite.

She always spoke in hushed tones about nature's beauty. When they were young women, Granny and her sister, Isabel Pifer, were tour guides on Longs Peak in Colorado—famous enough that their pictures are on display at the YMCA of the Rockies Museum in Estes Park, Colorado. They would head out from the YMCA camp at 3 A.M., leading hiking tours along the twenty-six-mile trek to Longs Peak summit and back. One of their favorite activities on the trail was to ask hikers to stop and listen to the sounds of nature. Granny taught us that, too.

As I stared at the Jack-in-the-pulpits, musing about Granny and her love of nature, I saw a small, round figure with a smiling face peeking out of the middle of the flower. Then another!

The flowers were filled with fairies! I smiled with glee and soon realized there were hundreds of fairies living among the wildflowers. They hopped on my leg, swarmed over my saddle, and covered the forest ground. These tiny fairies, about three to four inches high, overflowed with love and animation, and they quickly made friends with Astre and me.

I had always wished fairies and hobbits and elves were

real. I'd been plagued by self-doubt since I saw my first fairy at the corporate retreat. The doubts eased, but did not vanish entirely, when I talked with fairies in meditation. And now hundreds of them were playing with me as I sat on Astre and laughed with unabashed happiness. Seven fairies latched onto my tall leather riding boots and remained with us on our ride through the forest. I did not want to go too far away from their home, and after a while I attempted to drop them off, thanking them graciously for making their presence known.

Two fairies stayed with me after I brushed and groomed Astre and put her out in the field.

I spent the rest of the day in my office, feeling the fairies' presence as I worked. I tried to concentrate and often smiled as I experienced their love and gaiety as they ran up and down my body. As evening approached and I was still toiling, the fairies waved their tiny hands good-bye and said in their singsong manner, *"We will always be with you!"* I thanked them somewhat distractedly and remained at work for three more hours, pleased to be able to concentrate fully on my job.

A few days later, I received another clarifying meditation at home. I had journeyed into the sky among thousands of glistening stars. Hundreds of white meteors shot past me. Each star denoted a different dimension, another form of reality, a new realm of existence. I was moving fast and being shown how much more life was still left to experience.

"Who am I?" I asked. My heart was open to receive. I heard the answer right away and typed it out. The voice was unfamiliar: pleasant, feminine, and mighty.

"You are One and you are all. You are One with God and all of creation. We are all One. We are all parts of each and every being on Earth, within our own reality. Each one of us is a separate and unique being. We are all connected to the whole."

I reached for my beautiful, clear-white quartz crystal, grasped it firmly, and was imbued with timeless knowledge. I remembered who I was and who I am now.

I sank back into deep meditation and felt the core of one-ness, connectedness. I requested clarification about my name. I thought it was interesting that the fairies called me Becky, unlike Lot, who called me Rebekah—the same sound but a different spelling than my birth name, Rebecca.

I meditated on the names Becky, Rebecca, and Rebekah. Ancient wisdom seemed attached to the name Rebekah—it felt spiritual, connected to all, but I didn't feel ready to change the spelling of my name.

Introducing myself as Rebecca reminded me that when I did something wrong as a kid, my parents called me Rebecca instead of Becky. I didn't want to feel bad about myself by always calling myself Rebecca, though Rebecca was fine for formal occasions.

When I used the name Becky, I felt surrounded by new, lighthearted energy, not the old knowledge implied by the old-fashioned spelling, Rebekah. The energy was definitely different with each spelling. Which name should I use?

I raised my head and sat up straight, feeling incredibly conflicted about everything. I loved my daily talks with Lot, meeting the fairies, talking with Archangel Michael and SoJo. I had begun to see life through shining eyes of brilliance. Yet I was increasingly concerned that I was going crazy. Was I schizophrenic? Was I experiencing a drug-induced flashback, even though I hadn't drunk or smoked in years? Why was this happening?

Multiple times each day, I questioned the reality of... I did not even know what to call it... my spiritual enlightenment? At the same time, I had never felt more alive, more in control, and more at peace with myself. I was happier and calmer than ever.

Schizophrenia would mean that I was not grounded in reality. As a Fellow of the American Occupational Therapy Association, I had studied mental health, including schizophrenia and other mental illnesses, for many years. I could distinguish between appropriate and inappropriate behavior and felt that I did know what was "real."

But what is reality?

I owned a successful business, had a staff of more than 150 people, and was easily able to distinguish workplace activities from my meditative experiences.

Was one reality more real than the other? Or were both realities real? If I were going crazy—which, frankly, I did not think I was—then why was this occurring?

My bookshelves overflowed with hundreds of apparently true stories about people who had experienced similar forms of reality expansion, spiritual communication, and after-death communication. Maybe my constant reading about past lives, communication with people who had passed on, and the consideration of different forms of reality had allowed me to experience similar concepts. Was I creating this new reality myself? I had never imagined anything remotely like these adventures, and I questioned whether my mind was broad enough to make it all up.

I shared my concerns with my longtime friend Sue Apter. We had been friends since BK—before kids—and she is very grounded in reality. She is also a social worker who often counsels people dealing with psychiatric issues. Sue had heard about my adventures since the beginning, and she listened patiently now while I tried to explain my misgivings, despite the joy and sense of rightness that spiritual communication brought me. She asked questions to clarify—or perhaps diagnose—and I answered as best I could.

Finally, she said, "Becky, you are not crazy. A bit unusual, but not schizophrenic or psychotic. I don't mind listening to your experiences—in fact, I enjoy it. I have no desire to journey myself, but there is no problem with your sharing your adventures with me, although I encourage you to be careful who you tell."

I tried hard to follow her advice... most of the time.

✳ *Illumination* ✳

Trust yourself. Be open to receive.

Use support from your family and friends if you need emotional assistance and love. Listen to the people you most admire, but remember: If you truly feel you are moving forward on the correct path, there is no need to give your power away and acquiesce.

There are several alternative or complementary health techniques that incorporate the concepts of energy work. If energy work interests you, consider becoming certified in Reiki[41] or Healing Touch[54, 55]. Explore yoga[56], shiatsu[57], tai chi[58], mindfulness[59], or other spiritual or new-age modalities you feel drawn to learn about. All these complementary practices facilitate awareness of energy's spiritual benefits. Each path helps you learn more about yourself and your place in the universe.

Allow yourself to be open to life's many offerings, and you will receive what you need. Believing that you can interact with spiritual entities is the first step to successful communication.

There are many spiritual centers around the country that offer hundreds of mind-expanding courses every year[60-62]. Many communities offer local continuing education programs taught by a variety of spiritual practitioners. Health food stores often list local workshops on their bulletin boards. These are all options for learning more. If their offerings resonate with you, try them out and see what you discover. And be sure to take a look at the books listed in the Resources section of this book.

Enjoy the journey!

✳ *Chapter 9* ✳

Life and Death (JUNE)

All endings are also beginnings.
We just don't know it at the time.

—MITCH ALBOM

I gazed outside, staring through Nancy's windows. I needed assurance that David's passage served some ultimate purpose, that it was not meaningless. "Trust the information you receive," Nancy said. "Do not be afraid to express it. 'Trust in spirit' means having total confidence that you'll receive what you need."

I knew she was right. The spiritual messages I'd received had been life-changing. I still questioned my sanity, but deep inside I knew that David was alive, just living in a different dimension. Plus I was convinced that multiple spirit beings wanted their presence known and would communicate with us if we acknowledged the possibility of their existence.

The phenomena that had entered my life in the nine months since David's passing were undeniable, yet going public with this knowledge scared me to my very core.

What would people think? How would they perceive me once I share my deep understanding that we are all linked in a common earthly existence? That there is tremendous potential for life lessons to occur if we pay attention to messages from spirit? That life is not as we discern on the surface, but filled with multidimensional layers of existence, all accessible to us through meditation, energy work, time spent in nature, and myriad other ways *if* we believe, *if* we acknowledge the possibility that life continues forever?

* * *

As I write this, it's been twenty years since David's death catapulted me into spiritual exploration. Every day, I recall Nancy's advice to trust in spirit and her counsel to "surround yourself with light and love before communicating with spirit guides." I've learned that positive, insightful enlightenment will occur when I ask for my highest good while visualizing light and love. Spirits have not imposed themselves unless I have been open to receive them. In all these years, I've had to send spiritual beings away only three or four times.

When I do find energy that is incompatible with mine, I use two techniques that Nancy taught me. The first is to simply physically leave the area. The second is to surround myself with an egg-shaped container of clear glass. This strong, transparent shield allows me to see out but prevents unwanted energy from entering. I can increase or decrease the depth of the shield through visualization, depending on the intensity of the situation. I rarely use shields, as I want to experience all sensations while continuing to grow and learn. Yet shielding does protect me from unwanted emotional angst and allows me to control the information I receive.

During the session when Nancy and I talked about trust,

I lounged in her comfy sitting-room chair and shared some recent experiences.

I had discovered a wellness conference organized by occupational therapist Michael Pizzi, held in Washington, D.C. The conference seemed legitimate and credible because two occupational therapists and a host of psychologists, neurologists, physicians, social workers, and nurses were presenters. Michael also offered a two-day preconference class on Reiki Levels I and II, taught by another occupational therapist, Ann Marie McClintock.

When I first arrived and saw Michael, I asked him to call me by my formal first name and my husband's last name: Rebecca Clausen. Michael looked at me quizzically but agreed. I suspect he thought I was being overly dramatic, but I knew I needed the safety of anonymity.

I loved learning about Reiki: The hand positions, experiential practice, and philosophy were stimulating and satisfying. The fact that Reiki was taught by an OT helped me accept the principles and gave me confidence to attend the rest of the conference.

A photo booth caught my eye as I entered the vendor section on the first day of the conference itself. The vendor was demonstrating Kirlian photography[63], which claimed to create images of auras, the energy fields that surround our bodies. I questioned the validity of this concept but thought it would be fun to experience. I stepped into the photo stall and had my picture taken. I was surprised to see that part of the white-colored aura around my head was missing. The face staring back at me from the photo looked nervous and skeptical. I put the picture in my pocketbook and forgot about it.

Over the next three days, I attended numerous insightful workshops on shiatsu, kinesiology, meditation, crystal energy, and vibrational sound healing. I met dozens of professionals, all of whom were exploring the relationship between spirituality and health care. My fears about my sanity decreased significantly.

I walked past the Kirlian photography booth at the end of the conference and decided to have my picture taken again. This time, the aura around my head was filled in completely, and I was smiling and relaxed! In just three days, my energy had changed dramatically. I'd felt that shift, and seeing it reflected in the Kirlian images was wonderful and affirming.

I practically skipped toward Michael to express my sincere appreciation for this magnificent conference. I showed him the "before and after" pictures and said he could now call me Becky Austill-Clausen, rather than Rebecca Clausen, because I felt much more comfortable with who I was. Michael gave me a big bear hug, and we promised to stay in touch. I came home refreshed and filled with renewed vigor to continue meditation and shamanic journeying.

A few days later, as I looked fondly at my Reiki I and Reiki II certificates, Ken asked me to give him Reiki. We entered our guest bedroom, where I'd temporarily located a space to provide Reiki to family, friends, and clients. My new portable massage table was beside the double bed. A multi-hued blanket covered the soft green cushioned treatment table, and a small colorful pillow rested at the head.

Ken stared at the floor-to-ceiling bookshelves covering three of the four walls. The shelves were packed with more than a thousand books on spirituality. Interspersed were thirty of David's books that I had inherited when he passed.

Ken (fully clothed, as is typical in Reiki) clambered onto the massage table, relaxed on his back, and closed his eyes.

I began by asking for Ken's highest good to surround him and requested the presence of his spirit guides and mine. I took a deep, meditative breath and placed my hands lightly on each side of his head, cradling his crown between my hands. I visualized the powerful Reiki symbol for clarity and sent him Reiki energy filled with love. I trusted in the spirits to guide me when it was time to change my hand location as I slowly moved my Reiki-attuned palms over his eyes. Ken's body easily accepted Reiki's universal energy, and I felt him relax deeply. When I sent Reiki to Ken's throat and then his heart, his eyes popped open and darted around the ceiling. A brilliant smile lit up his face. After a few minutes, I softly asked, "Kenny, what are you looking at?"

He laughed and pointed. "Uncle David is here! He is doing somersaults on the ceiling!" I quickly looked up. David was nowhere that I could see, but apparently he was visible to Ken. I continued to provide Reiki while Ken's eyes flickered from side to side. After ten minutes of animated eye movement, Ken tilted his head sideways, lifted up his right hand, and waved. "Uncle David just waved to me from the door. He's leaving now." Ken closed his eyes, took a deep breath, and our Reiki session continued for another fifteen minutes.

I handed Ken a glass of water as he sat on the side of the massage table, swinging his legs.

"How do you feel?" I asked.

He smiled and pointed to the bookshelf directly beside us. "Uncle David showed me some of his books to read."

"Really? Which ones?"

Ken jumped off the table and pointed to a Piers Anthony science fiction book.

YES! I thought. That was one of David's books!

Then Ken strode to the bookshelf across the room and chose a second Piers Anthony book. It, too, was David's. He darted to a third bookshelf, stood high on his tiptoes, and touched a third book, also by Piers Anthony, also David's.

"Yes, Ken, these are all Uncle David's books. It's great you could see him!"

Ken beamed. "Thanks, Mom!" He gave me a deep, joyful hug, then ran outside to play with Ryan and their friends.

I couldn't have asked for a better validation for my spiritual explorations than what I'd just observed. When I told Nancy about the wellness conference and Ken's innocent visualization, she expressed delight at my growing confidence. We agreed that tapping into spiritual energy had certainly expanded my awareness about life's possibilities—those possibilities, I was beginning to understand, were limitless.

One of the conference workshops mentioned past lives. As I lay down on Nancy's massage table, I asked her opinion about past life regression. Agreeing that it was possible, she shifted quickly into instructor mode.

"Set your intention to have a past life experience. Open up all your chakras and be prepared to take a journey. You have the wisdom needed to balance the information you will receive from another dimension."

Fantastic! Nancy was going to assist me with accessing my own past life! I took a deep, centering breath and concentrated on her instructions. I consciously felt each of my seven chakras expand, opening like flowers reaching toward the bright morning sun. I set my intention to have a past life experience that was for my highest good. My heart was filled with love.

Nancy's calm voice continued. "We can use our intentions to manifest what we want here on Earth. Earth is a safe place; we can go into the Earth, to the center of the Earth if we want. To experience a past life, we travel to the Garden of Transition."

I imagined a garden filled with old-fashioned heirloom flowers. Pale pink roses blossomed with morning dew. Violet snapdragons bent their tiny heads toward the earth. Light blue hydrangeas waved in the soft breeze. I felt safe and protected.

Nancy directed me to an opening in the stone wall at the garden corner. "If you want to travel to a particular lifetime or time frame, be specific with your intention. If you desire information about a person, like Jeff or your parents, think about them. Spiritually, ask their permission to be present and accept the answer without question. If they want to join you, hold hands and go through the opening together. If they do not want to be involved, let them go."

I had no need to control what information I received, so I didn't ask for specifics. I accepted that what I learned was for my own betterment and self-actualization. I was excited and a bit nervous. I wondered, *What will I see?*

"Look down when you walk through the opening in the garden wall, and step onto the ground. It's good to be grounded when you travel to other lifetimes," Nancy coached.

"Gaze carefully at your feet. Notice if they seem larger or smaller, what footwear you have on, or if you have bare feet. You may observe a different skin color. You could be a female or a male. Do not try to change anything about your vision. Just let it be."

I saw an eighteen-year-old boy with tousled blond hair tumbling to a few inches below his shoulders. He wore wide, long, flowing pants, no shirt, and no shoes. I felt a deep heart-to-heart connection with this fellow as I observed his steady, controlled demeanor. I realized I was looking at myself in a different lifetime.

Nancy spoke gently, clearly on a mission to help me relive a past life experience. "Ask yourself, how are you feeling? Look out over the horizon, study the landscape, and ask this person, yourself, to describe what he or she sees. Try to receive information about the country where you are. Do not force anything. Just let it come. Listen carefully and accept the messages without censure."

Wispy steam rose from golden desert sand as rivulets of sweat traced my naked shoulders. The ever-present sun beat down on me. My body, strengthened by daily menial labors that helped provide my family with shelter from the heat and oppression of slavery, was lithe, muscular. I stared at the horizon, and a knowing rose up in my soul. I was living in Egypt.

"Look around." Nancy's familiar tone was comforting and reassuring. "You may start to see people you know. Ask questions without judgment. Pay attention to buildings and locations." I shifted inside this youth, consciously aware of my emotions and thoughts. I felt an intimacy, a sense of belonging that comes from living in a place for years. This desert oasis was my home.

I ducked gracefully inside the dark opening of a large pyramid, the centerpiece of my master's estate. My lean teenage body sprinted up the spiral of even stone steps that ended in a narrow stone alcove on the second floor. I surreptitiously looked around, breathing hard. I was alone. I didn't want to be beaten up again by the tyrant, my sovereign.

I stepped toward a flat rock jutting out from the wall; it was my writing surface. I picked up a long reed brush and carefully dipped it into a viscous black liquid, being careful to leave no blots on the papyrus. I wrote with smooth, precise strokes, inscribing payment figures from tenants who bought the master's crops from his many fields harvested by slaves. I had a good memory for numbers and had scribed for the master for two years. I preferred scribing to endless physical labor.

I calmly listened to Nancy while I watched myself, seemingly from a distance, carefully recording crop tallies beside each tenant's name. "Ask to go to a very special event during this time, something that is significant for your highest good. Remember that this has happened to you before, and you are just being shown again what occurred. You will not be hurt.

Pay attention. Follow your instincts and guidance. It is very common for people to become emotional when they are in another lifetime, so stay with the feeling."

Suddenly the scene changed, and my eighteen-year-old male self was now flying through the air! My arms were spread wide away from my body as I soared. I was not alone and felt others beside me. I did not recognize their shape or demeanor but knew they were friendly.

I saw a gigantic commotion in the town square below and circled closer for a better look. I noticed stone gallows and lots of people shouting and yelling as a male body hung dead, swinging in the breeze.

I looked closely at the corpse and immediately halted, startled. That body was me! But wait, I was still alive, gliding through the air!

I continued to exist! My physical form had been killed, but my spirit lived. The essence of me remained.

I was imbued with a sense of vibrancy, a feeling of wonder and joyous understanding that my body can die but my soul lives forever.

"Why have I been killed?" I asked. Quickly my guides answered.

"Your master said you were stealing. He asked you to make fake entries in the ledger so he could collect more money from the tenants. You changed some numbers to assist the slaves and got caught. You were hanged because you refused to comply with his wishes, and to serve as an example that the master's word is law."

This behavior made sense, and I was proud of my integrity. I swooped and swirled and flowed with the wind, feeling more alive and vibrant than ever. I stared again at my dead body blowing in the breeze and marveled that I still had life.

Seeing my death solidified my understanding that our

soul, our spirit, or whatever we want to call it—our essence—will continue forever, regardless of the state of our corporeal bodies. I experienced a mushrooming realization, a deep knowing that embraced the very core of who I am.

Physical death represents only a diminishment of physicality, not the extinguishment of who we are. Life does not end when our bodies expire. We continue to exist in a different realm without the clunkiness of our bodies.

I will never again be afraid of dying.

I will live for eternity.

Illumination

What do you think about death? Do you think our souls live on once our bodies expire? I was never sure what I thought until I began experiencing Edward's and David's presences after they had passed from this earth. Then the fairies came, and Lot and SoJo and Archangel Michael, and life became dramatically different from what I originally perceived.

During my first year of experiential journeys, I regularly questioned my sanity. Going frequently to professional conferences and new-age workshops, reading dozens of books that validated my metaphysical experiences, and continuing my exploration with Nancy allowed me to accept the eternity of life.

What do you believe?

Give yourself permission to explore whatever avenue feels right to you, as long as you surround yourself with love and ask for your highest good.

Savor the moments.

✳ *Chapter 10* ✳

David Returns (JULY)

*What lies behind us and what lies before us are
small matters compared to what lies within us.*

—HENRY STANLEY HASKINS

Summer, my favorite season of the year, arrived. The air
was warm and the trees sparkled in bright green patterns. I
was eager to go camping at our annual Cape Cod Austill family and friends reunion. Yet this summer would be different;
David wouldn't be with us.

Our family's camping history is told and retold around
blazing fires each August. It all started with Granny and
Gramps. They loved to travel and would often take their two
young sons, Dad and his brother Allen, camping. As a kid, I,
too, cuddled in the back of Granny's Volkswagen car camper,
nestled between soft brown bear rugs. I was always thrilled
when we parked beside a field of wildflowers. Pam, David, and
I would tumble out and run gleefully as Granny cooked a deli-

cious lunch on the camper's built-in one-burner stove, regally positioned to the right of the heavy sliding car door.

Back when I was only a year old, my parents decided to try camping on their own. They were working as camp counselors in Michigan and discovered a lovely lakeside campground in Sudbury, Ontario, in Canada, for their first camping adventure. Gramps loaned them the little green pup tent he had used as an Army chaplain while stationed in the Aleutian Islands in Alaska.

Dad loves to tell the story. "An older couple taught us the ropes," he rumbles in his deep baritone. "We boiled water in a tiny pan on a one-burner stove to warm Becky's glass bottle of milk. A train whistle blew throughout the night, waking us all up, and Becky would scream. When we rose in the morning, our water was frozen solid."

Despite the challenges, my parents loved the freedom and peace of camping. That first summer, they also camped on the shores of Lake George, New York, which reinforced their love of the activity. The next summer, they invited Uncle Allen and Aunt Joan to join them at Nickerson State Park in Cape Cod. Uncle Allen used to say he only wanted to stay in hotels, but after experiencing just one day of camping, he exclaimed gleefully, "This is the life!" Our families' yearly Cape Cod adventures had begun.

Dad had four weeks off each year, and he used them all at once in the summer. I have wonderful childhood memories of playing in the sand with my trucks at our campsite, high on a hill at the end of a little cul-de-sac.

After four weeks at Nickerson, we packed up our gear and drove thirty minutes to camp further down the Cape for another two weeks at the Audubon wildlife sanctuary in Wellfleet, Massachusetts. Dad would join us for a few days during the week. We could not have open fires on Audubon land, but we were totally entranced by hiking the park's trails, catching butterflies in the field, petting the tame horse, and attending naturalist activities designed for kids.

Every summer, our cousins Randy, Chris, and Lori and their awesome foreign exchange student from Morocco, Mohamed Bahouali, camped with us. Mohamed was essentially adopted by Uncle Allen and Aunt Joan's family and lived with them in New Jersey from the sixth grade on.

Our camping summers were glorious, filled with outdoor fun, freedom, and adventure. Every day we bodysurfed in the ocean and cleaned off the salt by swimming in one of the many freshwater lakes at Nickerson. At night, we cooked out under the stars, ate s'mores, sang folk songs, and slept in our tents. As our families grew, we upgraded from Granny and Gramps' big green Army tents to pop-up trailers. We still used our huge canvas tarps, which provided a nice homey spot to relax in, as well as shelter from inclement weather.

We kept up the two-week camping vacation tradition as we grew to adulthood. Each day begins with a morning dip: At 8 A.M., we rendezvous at the "morning dip site" and trudge down the hill to the kettle pond, a lake formed by glaciers with no outside streams to feed it. Every night is a glorious happy hour, where everyone brings food to share, and we regale each other with life updates, reminisce about old times, party on the beach, have huge bonfires, and (of course) eat s'mores. The summer before David passed, our yearly gathering had expanded to include eighteen campsites packed with friends, extended family, and a band!

That last summer, David and Loreen did their best to remain positive and upbeat, even though he was weak and could not swim in his beloved ocean.

I trudged slowly past David's favorite campsite, number fourteen, and stopped, remembering his gold-colored tent big enough for four people. I pictured his meticulously erected tarp, the camp chairs in a semicircle around the fire pit. His big, booming laugh reverberated in my memory as I recalled his making exquisite cocktails for Loreen and himself, then sitting around the campfire, watching flames spout high into the air from wood he'd chopped himself. I remembered that his stomach shunt provided pain medicine every few hours.

An empty hole gnawed at my soul. I reached into my jeans pocket and caressed David's quartz crystal, which I'd brought for comfort. I raised the lightweight crystal to my heart and sent waves of love to my brother, my tears splattering the ground, forming tiny indentations in the soft brown dirt.

As I walked slowly away, my body shriveled with sorrow, I realized that my head was not pounding with spasms. I'd worked long hours before vacation in order to leave everything in the capable hands of my office staff, but for the first time since I'd started working twenty years ago, I didn't have a headache as my vacation began. I knew this wasn't a coincidence. I cupped David's crystal protectively in my palm, then slid it back into my pocket.

The next day, Jeff and I clasped each other's hands loosely as we ambled along the seacoast at Coast Guard Beach in Eastham, Massachusetts. Waves crashed like a thousand cymbals against the shore, the sharp notes of a seagull's caw split the air, and hundreds of rocks tinkled a primal melody as huge waves washed them back into the ocean. Wet sand oozed between my toes, and blazing sun warmed my body. My heart overflowed with love.

"Hi, Becky! I'd like to come to happy hour tonight!"

David's voice startled me—his voice was in my mind. My eyes grew wide with excitement.

"Hi, David! It's great to hear from you! How are you?" I sent my message telepathically, glowing joyfully as I silently formed the name *David* with my mouth and pointed to my head, sharing with Jeff that David was there.

David did not answer me directly but repeated the message that he wanted to come to happy hour. My heart burst with love as tears formed in my weary eyes. It had been a long ten months without him. I missed him more than I'd ever thought possible.

I rapidly tried to figure how David could come to happy hour and decided it would work out somehow. I had learned to trust in the universe, to trust my instincts, and David's request felt right to me. It certainly would be a first for the Austill family and friends reunion to have a deceased relative come to happy hour!

I explained David's request to Jeff. "How is this going to happen?" he asked.

"I have no idea. I'm just going with the flow." Jeff caught my hand and squeezed reassuringly. Whatever happened, he'd be there for me, with me. We strolled back to where our group lounged on vibrant towels under a cluster of umbrellas near the tall white lifeguard chair.

Dad rose to greet us as we approached. I was too excited to stay quiet, and I called out, "Dad! David was just here and wants to come to happy hour tonight!"

"David was here? What do you mean?"

"He was talking with me and says he wants to come to happy hour," I said, passionate but a bit hesitant. Would Dad accept David's request? "He seemed lonely and wants to be with us."

Dad rubbed the top of his tanned head, a combination of thinking and stalling for time. "Let me talk with your mother about this," he said. He slowly walked toward Mom, who was sitting a few yards from the ocean, relaxing in her bright red-and-gold beach chair, her long legs digging deep into the wet sand. She turned to smile at Dad, her lips plastered in white zinc lip balm.

Dad and Mom had listened compassionately to my stories about communicating with David all year. I was not sure I could have survived the experiences without their support. I would just have to wait.

I sent a quick thought to David that Dad was talking with Mom and would get back with me soon. Upon later reflection, I realized that David probably already knew what Dad was doing, but I didn't want to take any chances that our spiritual communication would wane.

David left my mind, yet his energy imprint engulfed me. I was thrilled he had come to visit while we were on the Cape.

It was time for lunch. Jeff and I reached for our picnic bag simultaneously, laughing when our fingers bumped into each other at the zipper. We'd splurged on "lobstah" rolls for ourselves and the boys. Eating lobster on the beach was a special treat. I kept quiet about David's presence and reminded myself to be patient. I had to wait for Dad's answer.

Finally he came over and said, "Can I speak with you for a minute, Becky?"

I smiled at Dad, and we walked away from the crowd.

"Your mother and I feel it may be a bit uncomfortable for some people to have David come to happy hour, but we would like to ask you to have a service, or whatever you want to call it, after happy hour."

"OK, Dad, that sounds fine."

"I have a few places in mind. Why don't you announce at happy hour your intention to have a remembrance of David afterward, and then whoever wants to be present can come?"

"Sure. Let's look at your locations when we get back to the campground."

I was not intending to have a service, but since Dad *is* a minister, it made sense that he and Mom would suggest one.

"Give my love to David, and your mother's, too."

"I will, Dad! I certainly will." I smiled brightly at him and sauntered back to Jeff with a grin. I told him the plan.

"I have no idea exactly what I'll do, but I guess I'll serve as a medium for David." I had never done this with a group before, and never with any of my relatives except Jeff, Ken, and Ryan.

Jeff noticed my nervousness poking through my excitement and said, "Becky, you talk with David, Lot, and the fairies all the time when I'm with you. You will be fine."

I gave him a lopsided smile, hoping—trusting—that he was right.

I contacted David and shared the news. At first he seemed a bit disappointed but quickly warmed up to the plan.

The rest of the day passed in a flurry. Soon Dad and I were driving to places in our campground that I had never visited. He showed me two locations in the woods that he thought would be nice for a "service for David." Each site was fine, but not exactly right. Dad mentioned one more spot but warned that it was very secluded and a bit hard to reach.

In silence, we drove down a winding, tree-shrouded dirt road. We were the only ones there. The serenity was profound. Birds twittered in the trees. Sunlight peeking through forest growth cast multihued shadows on ferns dotting unseen paths. Finally, the road ended.

I climbed a gentle hill and gasped when I reached the top. We were looking out over a tranquil lake. Its surface sparkled in the glow of late afternoon.

David is a Pisces, the sign of the fish. He loved water. He also loved to camp in the woods.

"Dad, this is it! It's perfect!"

"Really? I thought you would like the second place we visited, with the shelter of the woods."

I assured Dad this was a great spot. He nodded in cautious agreement, and said, "I will be with you tonight, but I am not sure about Mom. She'll make her own decision."

"That's all right, Dad. Whoever wants to come, or not come, is fine with me."

Frankly, I still had no idea how I was going to do this, but I knew I could trust David and my guides to assist me. I turned again to the view of the beautiful lake.

"When did you find this place, Dad?"

"Years ago, when Mom and I first started camping at Nickerson. I've never seen anyone else here."

We spent a few more minutes enjoying the scene. As we headed back to get ready for happy hour, I sent love to David, blessing this spot with my mind while leaving my heart wide open. I was as ready as I could be to receive and share David's communication.

During happy hour, I cautiously announced to twenty family members and friends that I had learned how to talk with David since he passed. I quickly looked around to gauge their reactions. They gazed at me, simply waiting to hear what I would say next.

I took a deep breath and continued. I explained that David came to me at Coast Guard Beach that afternoon and wanted to join us, that Dad and I had found a lovely quiet spot where this might happen, and that we needed to drive to get there. We would leave at 7:30 P.M., and anyone who wanted to come would be welcome. And would they please bring chairs or something to sit on during this remembrance.

Some people looked skeptical, others seemed surprised. A few immediately chimed in with, "I'll come!"

By 7:30, nine people had gathered at Jeff's and my camp-site. Jiffy and John volunteered to watch Ken and Ryan along with their own two sons, Stephen and Matthew, at their camp-site. Pam and Bruce stayed back with their young son, Aaron. Mom stayed with Jiffy.

Dad took the lead. Jeff and I rode with him, and the others followed. It was dusk, the in-between twilight time, perfect for otherworldly communication.

We parked our cars and walked down the deserted road. Uncle Allen pushed Aunt Joan up the gentle hill in her wheel-chair. Once we reached the top, Mohamed set up his folding chair facing the lake. Uncle Allen placed Aunt Joan and her "chariot" beside Mohamed and locked the brakes. Mohamed opened up a chair for Allen and placed it next to Joan. Dad casually set up his chair near Allen. Jeff sat beside Dad, fol-lowed by our cousin Chris and his fiancée, Joelle. Bill Buchan, Jiffy's father-in-law, sat on the end next to Randy. They formed an informal semicircle, facing the lake.

I sat in my favorite dark green Coleman chair, my back to the lake, facing them.

I smiled at everyone and thanked them for coming. I took a deep breath and closed my eyes.

Immediately I sensed David's presence in my mind. He was very happy to be with us. I felt him send love to everyone present. David's love was so strong that it seemed like he was sending a strong, pulsing, soothing beacon of love to everyone in the campground.

I was a bit nervous—this was the first time I'd served as a medium for David in public—but I opened my mouth and started saying the phrases I heard in my mind. His comments were calm and thoughtful; he had remarks for everyone pres-ent. He asked about each person's family, job, and pertinent life events, whatever was relevant for that individual. I relayed his statements in the same normal conversational manner he would use if he were physically present. At one point, I peeked to make sure David was addressing each person there. Of course he was, and I quickly shut my eyes again to keep the connection strong.

I'd typed messages from Lot and other spirits for months. Sometimes Jeff would sit beside me and have me ask the guides questions. He always tried to "trip up the spirits," but each time they had an answer for Jeff that seemed reasonable.

This evening, though, was different. I was actually listening to David's voice in my head, saying out loud what I heard, and passing his messages to loved ones who were here with us.

The interaction I remember best was with Mohamed, who engaged in a brief dialogue with David.

"How are you doing, David? I miss smoking cigarettes with you around the fire."

David's response—"I miss you too, Mohamed"—was filled with a deep melancholy.

The intensity of David's angst was so profound that I almost lost connection with him as my own sorrow began to overwhelm me. But David's incredibly strong presence and the vitality of love sustained me and gave me strength to continue. I realized I could suppress my own emotions while maintaining the voice I heard in my head. It was almost like having two parts of my brain perform different acts at the same time: One side spoke David's words and the other watched from afar, disconnected emotionally from the physical act of speaking.

I relayed David's messages of love to each person. He had no comment or censure for those not present; he understood. At last, he was silent.

I took a deep breath and opened my eyes, scanning faintly visible faces in the dark. I received tender smiles back from everyone.

I was stunned that this had worked so well.

"Let's all stand up and join hands," I suggested. "Fill your hearts with love. Visualize a huge white balloon ascending to David, loaded with love."

We rose and joined hands, forming a close-knit circle, smiling quietly at each other, filled with love. The soft blinks of fireflies punctuated the gentle darkness that surrounded us. Trees rustled as if settling for sleep. Crickets chirped in subtle harmony.

"Let's all close our eyes, take a deep, heartfelt breath, and send David love now."

The power in our circle was immense. The energy was palpable. Pine needles, wispy ferns, and tall trees shimmered with it. Our hearts and souls joined in love for David.

Suddenly, a deafening screech broke the silence. All our eyes opened in shock.

A bellowing note, then another, shrieked in the dense forest.

Another screech pierced the night. Air whooshed to the left of me.

All of a sudden, I realized... bagpipes were playing!

I turned my head, listening hard, peering into the dark. A tallish, roughly middle-aged man stood to my left, about fifteen feet away, his back to the lake, barely visible. His fingers moved quickly over the chanter as the bagpipes bellowed and squealed, the large bag wheezing a steady rhythm of harsh wails. I stared in utter shock.

He was playing "Amazing Grace," the song we had sung at David's funeral. On bagpipes. In the middle of the woods. You've got to be kidding!

I burst into laughter.

"Becky, is this part of the show?" Aunt Joan's question floated up from her place in the circle. "Did you arrange this?"

I shook my head while tears—of disbelief, of hysterical

laughter, of gratitude—streamed from my eyes. David had always had a sense of humor. But my gosh, bagpipes in the middle of the forest? How did he ever think of that? We never heard bagpipes at the Cape. Our family does not play bagpipes at funerals or weddings. Bagpipe drones in Nickerson State Park? I was laughing so hard at the outrageousness of it that I couldn't speak.

The bagpiper finished playing one verse of "Amazing Grace" with a flourish and a slight bow. Wind rustled the trees again, and for a long moment, there was nothing but silence. Then we all erupted in animated chatter.

Chris and Dad walked over to talk with the bagpiper. I kept my distance but noticed that stickers from around the world covered his battered bagpipe case. I learned later from Chris that our musician just had a desire to walk down this deserted road at night to play his bagpipes for no particular reason.

I couldn't stop laughing at this incredible incongruity. David had just given us a remarkable validation that he was truly present. "Thank you, David!" I sent telepathically. His gaiety and joy were palpable as we connected once more. My soul rejoiced, exalting with love and admiration for my incredible brother, who had expanded my awareness and brought me so much joy and understanding.

We folded up our chairs, slid them into their nylon carrying bags, and heaved them over our shoulders. Mohamed pushed Aunt Joan's wheelchair over the soft, pine-needled ground. Flashlights clicked on as we left our circle of remembrance, the tiny beacons of light illuminating the forest above the still lake waters. Our chatter reverberated through the woods as we walked down the hill and along the path back to the cars.

I was the last to leave. My heart blazed with love. *Thank you, David, for being with us tonight and demonstrating your presence in such a profound way.* I walked behind the group, almost in a daze, listening to the spirited discussions about our otherworldly experience. When we returned to the campsites and shared what had happened, people were stunned. Many thought we were making up the night's adventures, but too many of us had experienced the excitement for it to be a fabrication.

The next morning, Dad said he was going to look for the bagpiper. I assured Dad he would not find him. I truly felt he was an angel, a messenger from David showing us that he really was alive—and would continue to be with us forever.

I thought back to the worst period of my life, ten months earlier.

Yet David's untimely passage introduced me to magical adventures that had pushed the boundaries of my wildest imagination. I never would have discovered multiple realities nor communicated with Lot, SoJo, Archangel Michael, the fairies, and of course, David, if he had not left me struggling to understand the meaning of his passage. I had uncovered the inner me, become more family-oriented, and stopped filling my life with aimless activities, trying to prevent boredom. I had reduced my workweek by about ten to twenty hours. (I still worked seventy to eighty hours, but that was better than a hundred!) My headaches had essentially stopped. I now found joy in the day-to-day pleasures of life.

My heart beamed love that soared toward David and showered him with gratitude. I was incredibly grateful for these remarkable metaphysical revelations.

Dad went to every site in the area but, as expected, never did find the bagpiper nor hear of anyone who played bagpipes in the entire campground.

✻ *Illumination* ✻

Everything in this story is real. It all happened to me twenty years ago. I am inordinately relieved to finally publicize these personal, life-changing events and look forward to hearing about your journeys of discovery.

What spiritual adventures have you had? Are there times in your life when you talked with loved ones who have passed on but maybe doubted their "realness" or the reality of the experience? Share your experiences with trusted loved ones. Ask for your highest good to be understood. I suspect you will be pleasantly surprised at the reaction.

Think about your family, your friends, your loved ones, and your pets. Do you feel as if you have known some of them forever? You probably have! Trust your instincts and travel within if you would like to know more.

It is estimated that fifty to one hundred million people in the United States have communicated with loved ones who have passed[64]. For some reason, people hardly ever speak about "talking with dead people." But an increasing number of movies, plays, television shows, psychics, and shamans are showcasing the ability to converse with spirits.

I never had the ability to communicate with spiritual

beings before David passed. If I can learn, so can you! There is nothing special about me that is any different from you. I share my story in hopes that it provides you with a basic structure and desire to learn how to communicate with loved ones and experience different forms of reality.

Follow your dream. Trust your instincts. Attend metaphysical workshops. Read new-age books. Go to spiritual conferences. Talk with like-minded individuals. See what happens.

Allow yourself time to observe what is right in front of your eyes. Go outside into nature, especially at dusk or dawn. Spend time with trees. Meditate. Journey. Express gratitude. Give yourself permission to take time for you. Be good to yourself.

Pay attention. Acknowledge the eternity of all life.

Above all, believe that you, too, can communicate with loved ones who have passed on. Connect with the spiritual entities that live all around us.

Have fun!

Endnotes

Authors with multiple book titles are recorded in chronological order as read by Rebecca Austill-Clausen.

1. Robertson, Janet. *The Magnificent Mountain Women: Adventures in the Colorado Rockies.* Lincoln, NE: Bison Books, 2003.

2. Melton, Jack R., and Lulabeth Melton. *YMCA of the Rockies: Reflections, Traditions & Vision.* Estes Park, CO: YMCA of the Rockies, 2006.

3. International Association for Near-Death Studies, Inc. (IANDS). Durham, NC 27705. http://iands.org.

4. Summer Rain, Mary. *Spirit Song: The Introduction of No-Eyes.* Charlottesville, VA: Hampton Roads Publishing, 1994.

5. Summer Rain, Mary. *Phoenix Rising: No-Eyes' Vision of the Changes to Come.* Charlottesville, VA: Hampton Roads Publishing, 1994.

6. Summer Rain, Mary. *Dreamwalker: The Path of Sacred Power.* Charlottesville, VA: Hampton Roads Publishing, 1993.

7. Summer Rain, Mary. *Phantoms Afoot: Helping the Spirits Among Us.* Charlottesville, VA: Hampton Roads Publishing, 2003.

8. Summer Rain, Mary. *Earthway: A Native American Visionary's Path to Total Mind, Body, and Spirit Health*. New York, NY: Atria Books, 1992.

9. Summer Rain, Mary. *Daybreak: The Dawning Ember*. Charlottesville, VA: Hampton Roads Publishing, 1994.

10. Summer Rain, Mary. *Soul Sounds: Mourning the Tears of Truth*. Charlottesville, VA: Hampton Roads Publishing, 1994.

11. Summer Rain, Mary. *Whispered Wisdom: Portraits of Grandmother Earth*. Charlottesville, VA: Hampton Roads Publishing, 1992.

12. Summer Rain, Mary. *Ancient Echoes: The Anasazi Book of Chants*. Charlottesville, VA: Hampton Roads Publishing, 1993.

13. Brown, Jr., Tom, and William Jon Watkins. *The Tracker: The Story of Tom Brown, Jr., as Told to William Jon Watkins*. New York, NY: Berkley Books, 1986.

14. Brown, Tom, Jr., and William Owen. *The Search: The Continuing Story of the Tracker*. New York, NY: Berkley Books, 2001.

15. Brown, Tom. *The Vision: The Dramatic True Story of One Man's Search for Enlightenment*. New York, NY: Berkley Books, 1988.

16. Brown, Tom. *The Quest: One Man's Search for Peace, Insight, and Healing in an Endangered World*. New York, NY: Berkley Books, 1991.

17. Roads, Michael J. *Talking with Nature: Sharing the Energies and Spirit of Trees, Plants, Birds, and Earth.* Tiburon, CA: H. J. Kramer, 1987.

18. Roads, Michael J. *Journey into Nature: A Spiritual Adventure.* Tiburon, CA: H. J. Kramer, 1990.

19. Roads, Michael J. *Journey into Oneness—Into a Timeless Realm.* Portland, OR: Six Degrees Publishing Group, Inc., 2015.

20. Save the Manatee Club. Maitland, FL 32751. http://www.savethemanatee.org.

21. Abraham, Edward A. *Freedom from Back Pain: An Orthopedist's Self-Help Guide.* Emmaus, PA: Rodale Press, 1986, 40.

22. Brennan, Barbara Ann. *Hands of Light: A Guide to Healing Through the Human Energy Field: A New Paradigm for the Human Being in Health, Relationship, and Disease.* New York, NY: Bantam Books, 1988.

23. Tolkien, J. R. R. *The Hobbit, or, There and Back Again.* Boston, MA: Houghton Mifflin Harcourt, 2012.

24. Tolkien, J. R. R. *The Fellowship of the Ring.* Boston, MA: Mariner Books, 2012.

25. Tolkien, J. R. R. *The Two Towers.* Boston, MA: Mariner Books, 2012.

26. Tolkien, J. R. R. *The Return of the King.* Boston, MA: Mariner Books, 2012.

27. Ingerman, Sandra. *Shamanic Journeying: A Beginner's Guide*. Boulder, CO: Sounds True, 2008.

28. Chopra, M.D., Deepak. http://www.deepakchopra.com.

29. Pachelbel, Johann, and Anastasi. *The Pachelbel Canon with Ocean Sounds*. Sausalito, CA: Real Music, 1990.

30. Andrews, Ted. *Animal-Speak: The Spiritual & Magical Powers of Creatures Great & Small*. St. Paul, MN: Llewellyn Publications, 2002.

31. Cunningham, Scott. *Cunningham's Encyclopedia of Crystal, Gem & Metal Magic*. St. Paul, MN: Llewellyn Publications, 2012.

32. Dolfyn. *Crystal Wisdom: Spiritual Properties of Crystals and Gemstones*. Oakland, CA: Earthspirit, 1989.

33. Hall, Judy. *The Crystal Bible: A Definitive Guide to Crystals*. Cincinnati, OH: Walking Stick Press, 2003.

34. The Foundation for Shamanic Studies: Mill Valley, CA 94942. https://www.shamanism.org.

35. Cowan, Tom. Highland, NY 12528. http://wp.riverdrum.com.

36. The Society for Shamanic Practice. Santa Fe, NM 87504. https://www.shamanicpractice.org.

37. Bey's Rock Shop. Bechtelsville, PA 19505. http://www.beysrockshop.com.

Endnotes

38. Keyes, Ken. *The Hundredth Monkey.* St. Mary, KY: Vision Books, 1981.

39. Sams, Jamie, and David Carson. *Medicine Cards: The Discovery of Power Through the Ways of Animals.* New York, NY: St. Martin's Press, 1999.

40. Masser, Michael, and Linda Creed. "The Greatest Love of All," recorded by Whitney Houston. Arista Records: February 14, 1985.

41. International Association of Reiki Professionals. http://www.iarp.org.

42. Eadie, Betty J., and Curtis Taylor. *Embraced by the Light.* New York, NY: Bantam, 1994.

43. Brady's Village Art Gallery and Rock Shop. Morgantown, PA 19543. http://jerebrady.com.

44. Andrews, Lynn V. *Medicine Woman.* New York, NY: TarcherPerigee, 2006.

45. Andrews, Lynn V. *The Flight of the Seventh Moon: The Teaching of the Shields.* San Francisco, CA: Harper San Francisco, 1985.

46. Andrews, Lynn V. *Jaguar Woman: The Wisdom of the Butterfly Tree.* New York, NY: J. P. Tarcher, 2007.

47. Andrews, Lynn V. *Star Woman: We Are Made from Stars and to the Stars We Must Return.* Boston, MA: Little Brown & Co., 1987.

48. Andrews, Lynn V. *Crystal Woman: The Sisters of the Dreamtime*. New York, NY: Warner Books, 1988.

49. Andrews, Lynn V. *Windhorse Woman: A Marriage of Spirit*. New York, NY: Grand Central Publishing, 1990.

50. Andrews, Lynn V. *Teachings Around the Sacred Wheel: Finding the Soul of the Dreamtime*. New York, NY: J. P. Tarcher, 2007.

51. Andrews, Lynn V. *The Woman of Wyrrd: The Arousal of the Inner Fire*. New York, NY: J. P. Tarcher, 2007.

52. Andrews, Ted. *Enchantment of the Faerie Realm: Communicate with Nature Spirits & Elementals*. St. Paul, MN: Llewellyn Publications, 2002.

53. Andrews, Ted. *How to Meet and Work with Spirit Guides*. St. Paul, MN: Llewellyn Publications, 2006.

54. Healing Touch International, Inc. dba: Healing Beyond Borders, Educating and Certifying the Healing Touch. Lakewood, CO 80228. http://www.healingbeyondborders.org.

55. Healing Touch Program. San Antonio, TX 78232. http://www.healingtouchprogram.com.

56. Yoga Journal. Cruz Bay Publishing, El Sequndo, CA 90245. http://www.yogajournal.com.

57. American Organization for Bodywork Therapies of Asia (AOBTA). AOBTA National Office, West Berlin, NJ 08091. http://www.aobta.org.

58. American Tai Chi and Qigong Association (ATCQA). Hemdon, VA 20171. http://www.americantaichi.org.

59. Mindfulness-Based Stress Reduction (MBSR, Jon Kabat-Zinn). Center for Mindfulness in Medicine, Health Care, and Society, University of Massachusetts Medical School, Worcester, MA 01655. http://www.umassmed.edu/cfm/.

60. Omega Institute for Holistic Studies. Rhinebeck, NY 12572. http://www.eomega.org.

61. Kripalu Center for Yoga & Health. Stockbridge, MA 01262. https://www.kripalu.org.

62. Esalen Institute. Big Sur, CA 93920. http://www.esalen.org.

63. Kirlian Cameras. Albany, NY 12207. http://www.kirlian cameras.com.

64. The After-Death Communication Project. Longwood, FL 32791. http://www.after-death.com.

Chapter Resources

I read nearly all the books listed below during David's illness, and they're still in my personal library. Their messages facilitated my initial ability to communicate with David and other spiritual entities.

Resources are organized categorically by chapter. Authors with multiple titles are listed chronologically in the order I introduce them within the book. This list is by no means exhaustive, but it does reproduce the beginning of my spiritual journey.

I encourage you to explore and expand on this information for your own self-discovery. Enjoy the adventure!

CHAPTER 1: TRANSFORMATION

After-Death Communication

Guggenheim, Bill, and Judy Guggenheim. *Hello from Heaven!: A New Field of Research, After-Death Communication, Confirms That Life and Love Are Eternal.* New York: Bantam Books, 1997.

Martin, Joel, Patricia Romanowski, and George Anderson. *Our Children Forever: George Anderson's Messages from Children on the Other Side.* New York: Berkley Trade, 1996.

Martin, Joel, and Patricia Romanowski Bashe. *Love Beyond Life: The Healing Power of After-Death Communications.* New York, NY: William Morrow Paperbacks, 2008.

Martin, Joel, Patricia Romanowski Bashe, and George Anderson. *We Are Not Forgotten: George Anderson's Messages of Hope from the Other Side.* New York, NY: Berkley Publishing Group, 1992.

---. *We Don't Die: George Anderson's Conversations with the Other Side.* New York, NY: Berkley Publishing Group, 2009.

Moore, Kirk. *Tara's Angels: One Family's Extraordinary Journey of Courage and Healing.* Tiburon, CA: H.J. Kramer, 1996.

Northrop, Suzane, and Kate McLoughlin. *The Seance: Healing Messages from Beyond.* New York, NY: Dell Books, 1995.

Schwimmer, George. *The Search for David: A Cosmic Journey of Love.* Charlottesville, VA: Heartsfire Books, 1996.

Autobiographical Spiritual Transformation

Alexander, Karen. *A Gift from Daniel.* New York: Berkley Publishing Group, 1996.

Andrews, Lynn V. *Shakkai: Woman of the Sacred Garden.* New York, NY: Harper Perennial, 1993.

---. *Woman at the Edge of Two Worlds: The Spiritual Journey of Menopause.* New York, NY: Harper Perennial, 1994.

---. *Walk in Balance: Meditations with Lynn Andrews.* San Francisco, CA: Harper San Francisco, 1994.

---. *Dark Sister: A Sorcerer's Love Story.* New York, NY: HarperCollins Publishers, 1995.

---. *The Power Deck: The Cards of Wisdom*. New York, NY: TarcherPerigee, 2004.

---. *Love & Power: Awakening to Mastery*. New York, NY: TarcherPerigree, 2007.

---. *Tree of Dreams: A Spirit Woman's Vision of Transition and Change*. New York, NY: TarcherPerigree, 2007.

Brown, Jr., Tom, and William Jon Watkins. *The Tracker: The True Story of Tom Brown, Jr., as told to William Jon Watkins*. New York, NY: Berkley Books, 1986.

Brown, Jr., Tom, and William Owen. *The Search: The Continuing Story of the Tracker*. New York, NY: Berkley Books, 2001.

---. *The Vision: The Dramatic True Story of One Man's Search for Enlightenment*. New York, NY: Berkley Books, 1996.

---. *The Quest: One Man's Search for Peace, Insight, and Healing in an Endangered World*. New York, NY: Berkley Books, 1996.

---. *The Journey: A Message of Hope and Harmony for our Earth and our Spirits*. New York, NY: Berkley Books, 2002.

---. *Grandfather: A Native American's Lifelong Search for Truth and Harmony*. New York, NY: Berkley Books, 2001.

---. *Awakening Spirits: A Native American Path to Inner Peace, Healing, and Spiritual Growth*. New York, NY: Berkley Books, 1994.

---. *The Way of the Scout: A Native American Path to Finding*

Spiritual Meaning in a Physical World. New York, NY: Berkley Books, 1997.

Crowley, Jonette. *The Eagle and the Condor: A True Story of an Unexpected Mystical Journey.* Greenwood Village, CO: Stonetree Publishing, 2007.

Kraft, Dean, and Rochelle Kraft. *A Touch of Hope: The Autobiography of a Laying-on-of-Hands Healer.* New York: G.P. Putnam's Sons, 1998.

MacLaine, Shirley. *Out on a Limb.* Toronto, CAN: Bantam Books, 1986.

---. *Going Within.* Toronto, CAN: Bantam Books, 1990.

---. *It's All in the Playing.* Toronto, CAN: Bantam Books, 1988.

---. *Dancing in the Light.* Toronto, CAN: Bantam Books, 1986.

MacLaine, Shirley, and Albert Sole. *The Camino: A Journey of the Spirit.* New York, NY: Atria Books, 2001.

Summer Rain, Mary. *Spirit Song: The Introduction of No-Eyes.* Charlottesville, VA: Hampton Roads Publishing, 1994.

---. *Phoenix Rising: No-Eyes Vision of the Changes to Come.* Charlottesville, VA: Hampton Roads Publishing, 1994.

---. *Dreamwalker: The Path of Sacred Power.* Charlottesville, VA: Hampton Roads Publishing, 1993.

---. *Phantoms Afoot: Helping the Spirits Among Us*. Charlottesville, VA: Hampton Roads Publishing, 2003.

---. *Earthway: A Native American Visionary's Path to Total Mind, Body, and Spirit Health*. New York, NY: Atria Books, 1992.

---. *Daybreak: The Dawning Ember*. Charlottesville, VA: Hampton Roads Publishing, 1994.

---. *Soul Sounds: Mourning the Tears of Truth*. Charlottesville, VA: Hampton Roads Publishing, 1994.

---. *Whispered Wisdom: Portraits of Grandmother Earth*. Charlottesville, VA: Hampton Roads Publishing, 1992.

---. *Ancient Echoes: The Anasazi Book of Chants*. Charlottesville, VA: Hampton Roads Publishing, 1993.

---. *Bittersweet*. Charlottesville, VA: Hampton Roads Publishing, 1995.

---. *The Visitation: An Archangel's Prophecy*. Charlottesville, VA: Hampton Roads Publishing, 1997.

---. *Millennium Memories: A Book of Days*. Charlottesville, VA: Hampton Roads Publishing, 1997.

---. *Fireside*. Charlottesville, VA: Hampton Roads Publishing, 1998.

---. *Eclipse*. Charlottesville, VA: Hampton Roads Publishing, 1999.

---. *The Singing Web*. Charlottesville, VA: Hampton Roads Publishing, 1999.

---. *Trined in Twilight*. Charlottesville, VA: Hampton Roads Publishing, 2000.

---. *Pinecones: Autumn Reflections*. Charlottesville, VA: Hampton Roads Publishing, 2001.

---. *Tao of Nature: Earthway's Wisdom of Daily Living from Grandmother Earth*. New York, NY: Fireside Books, 2002.

---. *Love Never Sleeps: Living at Home with Alzheimer's*. Charlottesville, VA: Hampton Roads Publishing, 2002.

---. *Woodsmoke: Autumn Reflections*. Charlottesville, VA: Hampton Roads Publishing, 2003.

Roads, Michael J. *Talking with Nature: Sharing the Energies and Spirit of Trees, Plants, Birds, and Earth*. Tiburon, CA: H. J. Kramer, 1987.

---. *Journey into Nature: A Spiritual Adventure*. Tiburon, CA: H. J. Kramer, 1990.

---. *Journey Into Oneness – Into a Timeless Realm*. Portland, OR: Six Degrees Publishing Group, 2015.

---. *Simple Is Powerful: Anecdotes For A Complex World*. Tiburon, CA: H. J. Kramer, 1991.

Wabun Wind. *Woman of the Dawn: A Spiritual Odyssey*. New York, NY: Prentice Hall Press, 1989.

Watson, Lyall. *Gifts of Unknown Things: A True Story of Nature, Healing, and Initiation from Indonesia's Dancing Island.* Rochester, VT: Destiny Books, 1991.

Wyllie, Timothy. *Dolphins, ETs & Angels: Adventures Among Spiritual Intelligences.* Santa Fe, NM: Bear & Co., 1993.

Death
Albom, Mitch. *Tuesdays with Morrie: An Old Man, a Young Man, and Life's Greatest Lesson.* New York, NY: Broadway Books, 2002.

---. *The Five People You Meet in Heaven.* New York, NY: Hachette Books, 2006.

---. *The Timekeeper.* New York, NY: Hachette Books, 2013.

Nhat Hanh, Thich. *No Death, No Fear: Comforting Wisdom For Life.* New York, NY: Riverhead Books, 2003.

Schwalbe, Will. *The End of Your Life Book Club.* New York, NY: Alfred A. Knopf, 2012.

Hospice
Hospice Directory by State. http://www.hospicedirectory.org.

National Association for Home Care and Hospice. Washington, DC 20003. http://www.nahc.org.

National Hospice and Palliative Care Organization. Alexandria, VA 22314. http://www.nhpco.org.

Chapter Resources

Love and Abundance

Helliwell, Tanis. *Embraced by Love: Poems*. Powell River, BC: International Institute for Transformation, 2008.

Roads, Michael J. *More Than Money, True Prosperity: A Wholistic Guide to Having It All*. Cleveland, OH: Silver Roads Publishing, 2004.

Roman, Sanaya, and Duanne R. Packer. *Creating Money: Attracting Abundance*. Tiburon, CA: H. J. Kramer, 2007.

Meditation, Channeling, and Mediumship

Cayce, Edgar, and Gladys Davis Turner. *Individual Reference File of Extracts from the Edgar Cayce Readings*. Virginia Beach, VA: Association for Research and Enlightenment, 1976.

Kenworthy, Donna. *A 1-900 Psychic Speaks*. Charlottesville, VA: Hampton Roads Publishing, 1998.

Marciniak, Barbara, and Tera Thomas. *Bringers of the Dawn: Teachings from the Pleiadians*. Santa Fe, NM: Bear & Co., 1993.

Nhat Hanh, Thich. *Peace Is Every Breath: A Practice for Our Busy Lives*. New York, NY: HarperOne, 2012.

Roman, Sanaya, and Duanne R. Packer. *Personal Power Through Awareness: A Guidebook for Sensitive People*. Tiburon, CA: H. J. Kramer, 1986.

---. *Spiritual Growth: Being Your Higher Self*. Tiburon, CA: H. J. Kramer, 1992.

---. *Opening to Channel: How to Connect With Your Guide.* Tiburon, CA: H. J. Kramer, 1993.

Roman, Sanaya, and Orin. *Living with Joy: Keys to Personal Power & Spiritual Transformation.* Tiburon, CA: H. J. Kramer, 2011.

Van Praagh, James. *Reaching to Heaven: A Spiritual Journey Through Life and Death.* New York, NY: Dutton, 1999.

---. *Talking to Heaven: A Medium's Message of Life After Death.* New York, NY: Dutton Signet, Penguin Putnam, 1999.

Walker, Ann. *The Stone of the Plough: The Search for the Secret of Giza.* Shaftesbury, Dorset: Element Books, 1997.

Near-Death Experiences and the Afterlife

Alexander, Eben. *Proof of Heaven: A Neurosurgeon's Journey into the Afterlife.* New York, NY: Simon & Schuster, 2012.

Brinkley, Dannion, and Paul Perry. *Saved by the Light: The True Story of a Man Who Died Twice and the Profound Revelations He Received.* New York, NY: Harper One, 2008.

---. *At Peace in the Light: The Further Adventures of a Reluctant Psychic Who Reveals the Secret of Your Spiritual Powers.* New York, NY: HarperCollins, 1995.

Burpo, Todd, and Lynn Vincent. *Heaven Is for Real.* Carol Stream, IL: Thomas Nelson, 2011.

Crawford, Jennifer Christine. *Spirit of Love: A Medium's Message of Life Beyond Death.* St. Paul, MN: Llewellyn Publications, 2002.

Kagan, Annie. *The Afterlife of Billy Fingers: How My Baby Brother Proved to Me There's Life After Death.* Charlottesville, VA: Hampton Roads Publishing, 2013.

Malarkey, Kevin, and Alex Malarkey. *The Boy Who Came Back from Heaven: A Remarkable Account of Miracles, Angels, and Life Beyond This World.* Carol Stream, IL: Tyndale House Publishers, 2010.

Morse, Melvin, and Paul Perry. *Closer to the Light: Learning from Children's Near-Death Experiences.* New York, NY: Villard Books, 1990.

Neal, Mary C. *To Heaven and Back: A Doctor's Extraordinary Account of Her Death, Heaven, Angels, and Life Again: A True Story.* Colorado Springs, CO: Waterbrook Press, 2012.

Piper, Don, and Cecil Murphey. *90 Minutes in Heaven: A True Story of Death and Life.* Grand Rapids, MI: Revell, 2004.

Pylant, Neal, and Christopher Pylant. *A Touch from Heaven: A Little Boy's Story of Surgery, Heaven, and Healing.* Shippensburg, PA: Destiny Image Publishing, 2013.

Sharp, Kimberly Clark. *After The Light: What I Discovered on the Other Side of Life That Can Change Your World.* Bloomington, IN: Universe, 2003.

---. *After The Light: The Spiritual Path to Purpose.* New York, NY: Avon Books, 1996.

Wills-Brandon, Carla. *A Glimpse of Heaven.* Hove BN3 3DH, United Kingdom: White Crow Books, 2012.

Organizations for Near-Death Experiences (NDE's), Near-Death-Like Experiences (NDLE's), and Spiritual Transformative Experiences (STE's)
American Center for the Integration of Spiritually Transformative Experiences (ACISTE). Little Elm, TX 75068. https://aciste.org.

International Association for Near-Death Studies, Inc. (IANDS). Durham, NC 27705-8878. http://iands.org.

CHAPTER 2: PASSAGES

Visionary Fiction for Self-Empowerment
Bach, Richard. *Jonathan Livingston Seagull*. Harper Element, Open Library, 2011.

---. *A Gift of Wings*. New York, NY: Dell, 1989.

---. *One: A Novel*. New York, NY: Dell, 1989.

---. *Running from Safety: An Adventure of the Spirit*. New York, NY: William Morrow & Co., 1994.

---. *Illusions: The Adventures of a Reluctant Messiah*. UK: Arrow Books Ltd., 2001.

---. *The Bridge Across Forever: A Love Story*. New York, NY: Dell Publishing, 2010.

---. *Biplane*, Kindle edition. New York, NY: Scribner, 2012.

---. *Nothing by Chance: A Gypsy Pilot's Adventures in Modern America*, Kindle edition. New York, NY: Scribner, 2012.

---. *Stranger to the Ground,* Kindle edition. New York, NY: Scribner, 2012.

---. *Messiah's Handbook: Reminders for the Advanced Soul.* Faber, VA: Rainbow Ridge, 2012.

---. *There's No Such Place as Far Away,* Kindle edition. Amazon Digital Services, LLC., 2015.

Joynes, Monty. *Naked into the Night: A Novel,* Kindle edition. Amazon Digital Services, LLC., 2013.

---. *Lost in Las Vegas,* Kindle edition. Amazon Digital Services, LLC., 2013.

---. *Save the Good Seed,* Kindle edition. Amazon Digital Services, LLC., 2013.

Martin, Stephen Hawley. *The Mt. Pelée Redemption: A Metaphysical Mystery.* Charlottesville, VA: Hampton Roads Publishing, 1998.

Summer Rain, Mary. *The Seventh Mesa: A Novel.* Norfolk, VA: Hampton Roads Publishing, 1997.

---. *Ruby: A Novel,* Kindle edition. Amazon Digital Services, LLC., 2011.

You Can Control Your Life and Heal Yourself

Andrews, Ted. *Magickal Dance: Your Body as an Instrument of Power.* St. Paul, MN: Llewellyn Publications, 1995.

---. *Sacred Sounds: Transformation Through Music & Word.* St. Paul, MN: Llewellyn Publications, 2001.

Byrne, Rhonda. *The Secret.* New York, NY: Atria Books, 2006.

---. *The Power.* New York, NY: Atria Books, 2010.

---. *The Magic.* New York, NY: Atria Books, 2012.

Cruden, Loren. *The Spirit of Place: A Workbook for Sacred Alignment: Ceremonies and Visualizations for Cultivating Your Relationship with the Earth.* Rochester, VT: Destiny Books, 2005.

McGaa, Ed. *Mother Earth Spirituality: Native American Paths to Healing Ourselves and Our World.* New York, NY: Harper-Collins Publishers, 1990.

Megre, Vladimir, and Leonid Sharashkin. *Anastasia: The Ringing Cedar Series, Book One.* Kahului, HI: Ringing Cedars Press, 2008.

---. *The Ringing Cedars of Russia: The Ringing Cedar Series, Book Two.* Kahului, HI: Ringing Cedars Press, 2008.

---. *The Space of Love: The Ringing Cedar Series, Book Three.* Kahului, HI: Ringing Cedars Press, 2008.

---. *Co-Creation: The Ringing Cedar Series, Book Four.* Kahului, HI: Ringing Cedars Press, 2008.

---. *Who Are We?: The Ringing Cedar Series, Book Five.* Kahului, HI: Ringing Cedars Press, 2008.

---. *The Book of Kin: The Ringing Cedar Series, Book Six.* Kahului, HI: Ringing Cedars Press, 2008.

---. *The Energy of Life: The Ringing Cedar Series, Book Seven.* Kahului, HI: Ringing Cedars Press, 2008.

---. *The New Civilisation: The Ringing Cedar Series, Book Eight.* Kahului, HI: Ringing Cedars Press, 2008.

---. *Rites of Love: The Ringing Cedar Series, Book Nine.* Kahului, HI: Ringing Cedars Press, 2008.

Mountain Dreamer, Oriah. *The Invitation: It Doesn't Interest Me What You Do For A Living. I Want to Know What You Ache For.* San Francisco, CA: Harper One, 2006.

---. *The Dance: Moving to the Rhythms of Your True Self.* San Francisco, CA: Harper One, 2006.

---. *The Call: Discovering Why You Are Here.* San Francisco, CA: Harper One, 2006.

Myss, Caroline M. *Spiritual Power, Spiritual Practice: Energy Evaluation Meditations for Morning and Evening.* Boulder, CO: Sounds True Audio, 2001.

Rathbun, Ron. *The Way Is Within: A Spiritual Journey.* Oceanside, CA: Quiescence Publishing, 2012.

Redfield, James. *The Celestine Prophecy: An Adventure.* New York, NY: Warner Books, 1997.

---. *The Tenth Insight: Holding the Vision*. New York, NY: Grand Central Publishing, 1998.

---. *The Secret of Shambhala: In Search of the Eleventh Insight*. New York, NY: Warner Books, 2001.

---. *The Twelfth Insight: The Hour of Decision*. New York, NY: Grand Central Publishing, 2012.

Rubin, Gretchen Craft. *The Happiness Project: Or Why I Spent a Year Trying to Sing in the Morning, Clean My Closets, Fight Right, Read Aristotle, and Generally Have More Fun*. York, NY: Harper Paperbacks, 2015.

Storm, Hyemeyohsts. *Seven Arrows*. York, NY: Ballantine Books, 1985.

Warter, Carlos. *Who Do You Think You Are?: The Healing Power of Your Sacred Self*. New York, NY: Bantam Books, 1999.

Weil, Andrew. *Eight Weeks to Optimum Health: A Proven Program for Taking Full Advantage of Your Body's Natural Healing Power*. New York, NY: Ballantine Books, 2007.

Ywahoo, Dhyani, and Barbara Du Bois. *Voices of Our Ancestors: Cherokee Teachings from the Wisdom Fire*. Boston, MA: Shambhala, 1987.

CHAPTER 3: SEARCH AND FIND

Chakras

Andrews, Ted. *How to Heal with Color*. St. Paul, MN: Llewellyn Publications, 2005.

Nature

Andrews, Ted. *Nature-Speak: Signs, Omens and Messages in Nature*. Jackson, TN: Dragonhawk, 2004.

Brown, Tom. *Tom Brown's Field Guide to the Forgotten Wilderness*. New York, NY: Berkley Books, 1987.

Brown, Tom, and Brandt Morgan. *Tom Brown's Field Guide to City and Suburban Survival*. New York, NY: Berkley Books, 1986.

---. *Tom Brown's Field Guide to Living with the Earth*. New York, NY: Berkley Books, 2002.

Klein, Tom. *Nature's Tranquility: Reflections and Insights*. Minnetonka, MN: Northword Press, 1999.

Roads, Michael J. *The Natural Magic of Mulch: Organic Gardening Australian Style*. Elwood, Victoria, Australia: Greenhouse Publications, 1989.

Van Lippe-Biesterfeld, Irene. *Dialogue with Nature*. Forres, Scotland: Findhorn, 1997.

Shamanism

Abelar, Taisha. *The Sorcerers' Crossing: A Woman's Journey*. New York, NY: Penguin, 1993.

Arvigo, Rosita, Nadine Epstein, and Marilyn Yaquinto. *Sastun: My Apprenticeship with a Maya Healer*. San Francisco, CA: Harper One, 1995.

Boulet, Susan Seddon. *Shaman: The Paintings of Susan Seddon Boulet*. San Francisco, CA: Pomegranate, 1994.

Castaneda, Carlos. *The Teachings of Don Juan; A Yaqui Way of Knowledge*. Oakland, CA: University of California Press, 2008.

---. *A Separate Reality: Further Conversations with Don Juan*. New York, NY: Pocket Books, 1982.

---. *Journey to Ixtlan: The Lessons of Don Juan*. New York, NY: Washington Square Press, 1991.

---. *The Power of Silence: Further Lessons of Don Juan*. New York, NY: Washington Square Press, 1991.

Cowan, Thomas Dale. *Fire in the Head: Shamanism and the Celtic Spirit*. San Francisco, CA: HarperSanFrancisco, 1993.

Crowley, Jonette. *The Eagle and the Condor: A True Story of an Unexpected Mystical Journey*. Greenwood Village, CO: Stonetree Publishing, 2007.

Harner, Michael J. *The Way of the Shaman*. San Francisco, CA: Harper & Row, 1990.

Ingerman, Sandra. *Welcome Home: Following Your Soul's Journey Home*. San Francisco, CA: Harper One, 1994.

---. *Soul Retrieval: Mending the Fragmented Self*. San Francisco, CA: Harper One, 2006.

Ingerman, Sandra, and Hank Wesselman. *Awakening to the Spirit World: The Shamanic Path of Direct Revelation*. Boulder, CO: Sounds True, 2010.

Madden, Kristin. *The Book of Shamanic Healing*. St. Paul, MN: Llewellyn Publications, 2002.

Meadows, Kenneth. *Shamanic Spirit: A Practical Guide to Personal Fulfillment*. Rochester, VT: Bear & Co., 2004.

Millman, Dan. *Way of the Peaceful Warrior: A Book That Changes Lives*. Tiburon, CA: H. J. Kramer, 2006.

---. *Sacred Journey of the Peaceful Warrior*. Tiburon, CA: H. J. Kramer, 2004.

---. *The Life You Were Born to Live: A Guide to Finding Your Life Purpose*. Tiburon, CA: H. J. Kramer, 1993.

Moss, Nan, and David Corbin. *Weather Shamanism: Harmonizing Our Connection with the Elements*. Rochester, VT: Bear & Co., 2008.

Perkins, John. *The World Is As You Dream It: Shamanic Teachings from the Amazon and Andes*. Rochester, VT: Destiny Books, 1994.

Roberts, Llyn, and Robert Levy. *Shamanic Reiki: Expanded Ways of Working with Universal Life Force Energy*. Winchester, UK: O Books, 2008.

Scully, Nicki, Linda Star Wolf, and Kris Waldherr. *Shamanic Mysteries of Egypt: Awakening the Healing Power of the Heart*. Rochester, VT: Bear & Co., 2007.

Starhawk. *The Spiral Dance: A Rebirth of the Ancient Religion of the Great Goddess*. San Francisco, CA: HarperSanFrancisco, 1999.

---. *Dreaming the Dark: Magic, Sex & Politics*. Boston, MA: Beacon Press, 1997.

---. *The Fifth Sacred Thing*. New York, NY: Bantam Books, 1994.

Tunneshende, Merilyn, and John Nelson. *Medicine Dream: A Nagual Woman's Energetic Healing*. Charlottesville, VA: Hampton Roads Publishing, 1996.

Warter, Carlos. *Recovery Of The Sacred: Lessons In Soul Awareness*. Deerfield Beach, FL: Health Communications, 1995.

Wesselman, Henry Barnard. *Spiritwalker: Messages from the Future*. New York, NY: Bantam Books, 1996.

---. *Medicinemaker: Mystic Encounters on the Shaman's Path*. New York, NY: Bantam Books, 1999.

---. *Visionseeker: Shared Wisdom from the Place of Refuge*. Carlsbad, CA: Hay House, 2002.

---. *The Bowl of Light: Ancestral Wisdom from a Hawaiian Shaman*. Boulder, CO: Sounds True, 2011.

---. *The Journey to the Sacred Garden: A Guide to Traveling in the Spiritual Realms*. Carlsbad, CA: Hay House, 2012.

Wesselman, Hank, and Jill Kuykendall. *Spirit Medicine: Healing in the Sacred Realms*. Carlsbad, CA: Hay House, 2004.

Whitaker, Kay Cordell. *The Reluctant Shaman: A Woman's First Encounters with the Unseen Spirits of the Earth*. San Francisco, CA: HarperSanFrancisco, 1991.

Shamanic Organizations and Workshops
Cowan, Tom. Highland, NY 12528. http://wp.riverdrum.com.

The Foundation for Shamanic Studies. Mill Valley, CA 94942. https://www.shamanism.org.

The Society for Shamanic Practice. Santa Fe, NM 87504. https://shamanicpractice.org.

Spirit Guides and Angels
Andrews, Ted. *How to Meet and Work with Spirit Guides*. St. Paul, MN: Llewellyn Publications, 2006.

Choquette, Sonia. *Ask Your Guides: Connecting to Your Divine Support System*. Carlsbad, CA: Hay House, 2007.

Taylor, Terry Lynn. *Messengers of Light: The Angels' Guide to Spiritual Growth*. Tiburon, CA: H. J. Kramer, 1993.

---. *Guardians of Hope: The Angels' Guide to Personal Growth*. Tiburon, CA: H. J. Kramer, 1993.

---. *Answers from the Angels: A Book of Angel Letters*. Tiburon, CA: H. J. Kramer, 1993.

---. *Creating with the Angels: An Angel-Guided Journey into Creativity*. Tiburon, CA: H. J. Kramer, 1993.

CHAPTER 4: FAIRY MAGIC

Dreams

Castaneda, Carlos. *The Art of Dreaming*. New York, NY: William Morrow Paperbacks, 2003.

Mellon, Emma. *Waking Your Dreams: Unlock the Wisdom of Your Unconscious*. Deerfield Beach, FL: Health Communications, 2006.

Summer Rain, Mary. *In Your Dreams: The Ultimate Dream Dictionary*. Charlottesville, VA: Hampton Roads Publishing, 2005.

Summer Rain, Mary, and Alex Greystone. *Mary Summer Rain on Dreams: A Quick-Reference Guide to Over 14,500 Dream Symbols*. Charlottesville, VA: Hampton Roads Publishing, 1996.

Fairies

Andrews, Ted. *Enchantment of the Faerie Realm: Communicate with Nature Spirits & Elementals*. St. Paul, MN: Llewellyn Publications, 2002.

Helliwell, Tanis. *Summer with the Leprechauns: A True Story*. Powell River, BC: Wayshower Enterprises, 2011.

---. *Pilgrimage with the Leprechauns: A True Story of a Mystical Tour of Ireland*. Powell River, BC: Wayshower Enterprises, 2010.

Kelly, Penny. *The Elves of Lily Hill Farm: A Partnership with Nature*. Lawton, MI: Lily Hill Publishing, 2005.

Matthews, John, and Matt Dangler. *Faeryland: The Secret World of the Hidden Ones*. New York, NY: Abrams, 2013.

Moorey, Teresa. *The Fairy Bible: The Definitive Guide to the World of Fairies*. New York, NY: Sterling, 2008.

Virtue, Doreen. *Fairies 101: An Introduction to Connecting, Working, and Healing with the Fairies and Other Elementals*. Carlsbad, CA: Hay House, 2011.

---. *Healing with the Fairies: Messages, Manifestations, and Love from the World of the Fairies*. Carlsbad, CA: Hay House, 2001.

---. *Magical Messages from the Fairies Oracle Cards. A 44 Card Deck and Guidebook*. Carlsbad, CA: Hay House, 2010.

Wright, Machaelle Small. *Behaving As If The God in All Life Mattered: A New Age Ecology*. Jeffersonton, VA: Perelandra, 1997.

Fairy Communication Workshops

Complementary Health Works (Rebecca Austill-Clausen, President). Downingtown, PA 19335. becky@comphealthworks. com, http://www.comphealthworks.com.

Findhorn Foundation. Visitor's Centre, The Park, Findhorn, IV36 3TZ, Scotland. https://www.findhorn.org.

International Institute for Transformation (Tanis Helliwell, Founder). Diamond Heart: Powell River, BC, Canada V8A 0M4. tanis@tanishelliwell.com, http://www.tanishelliwell.com.

CHAPTER 5: CRYSTAL ENERGY AND ANIMAL WISDOM

Animals

Andrews, Ted. *Animal-Speak: The Spiritual & Magical Powers of Creatures Great & Small.* St. Paul, MN: Llewellyn Publications, 2002.

---. *The Animal-Wise Tarot.* Jackson, TN: Dragonhawk Publishing, 1999.

---. *The Animal-Speak Workbook.* Jackson, TN: Dragonhawk Publishing, 2002.

---. *Animal-Wise: Understanding the Language of Animal Messengers and Companions.* Jackson, TN: Dragonhawk Publishing, 2010.

Brown, Tom. *The Science and Art of Tracking: Nature's Path to Spiritual Discovery.* New York, NY: Berkley Books, 1999.

Sams, Jamie, and David Carson. *Medicine Cards: The Discovery of Power Through the Ways of Animals.* New York, NY: St. Martins Press, 1999.

Animal Organization

Save the Manatee Club. Maitland, FL 32751. http://www.save themanatee.org.

Crystals

Cohen, Neil S. *Crystal Awareness Guide: The Transformational Properties of Gems and Minerals.* CA: Legion of Light Products, 1987.

Cunningham, Scott. *Cunningham's Encyclopedia of Crystal, Gem & Metal Magic.* St. Paul, MN: Llewellyn Publications, 2012.

Dolfyn. *Crystal Wisdom: Spiritual Properties of Crystals and Gemstones.* Oakland, CA: Earthspirit, 1989.

Hall, Judy. *The Crystal Bible: A Definitive Guide to Crystals.* Cincinnati, OH: Walking Stick Press, 2004.

Shapeshifting

Andrews, Ted. *The Art of Shapeshifting.* Jackson, TN: Dragonhawk Publishing, 2006.

CHAPTER 6: EXPLORATIONS

Time

Rechtschaffen, Stephan. *Time Shifting: Creating More Time to Enjoy Your Life.* New York, NY: Doubleday, 1996.

CHAPTER 7: DISCOVERY

Reiki, Healing Touch, and Therapeutic Touch

International Association of Reiki Professionals. http://www.iarp.org.

International Center for Reiki Training (William Lee Rand, Founder). Southfield, MI 48033. center@reiki.org, http://www. reiki.org

International Center for Reiki Training. *Reiki News Magazine.* Southfield, MI: Vision Publications, 1991.

Healing Touch International, Inc. dba: Healing Beyond Borders, Educating and Certifying the Healing Touch. Lakewood, CO 80228. http://www.healingbeyondborders.org.

Healing Touch Program. San Antonio, TX 78232. http://www. healingtouchprogram.com.

Krieger, Delores. *Therapeutic Touch Inner Workbook: Ventures in Transpersonal Healing.* Santa Fe, NM: Bear & Co., 1997.

Spiritual Philosophy
Carson, David. *Crossing into Medicine Country: A Journey in Native American Healing.* New York, NY: Arcade Publishing, 2014.

The Dalai Lama, and Rajiv Mehrotra. *In My Own Words: An Introduction to My Teachings and Philosophy.* Carlsbad, CA: Hay House, 2011.

Gendler, J. Ruth. *The Book of Qualities.* New York, NY: Perennial Library, 1988.

Gerber, Richard. *Vibrational Medicine: The #1 Handbook of Subtle-Energy Therapies.* Santa Fe, NM: Bear & Co., 2001.

Weil, Andrew. *Spontaneous Healing: How to Discover and*

Enhance Your Body's Natural Ability to Maintain and Heal Itself. New York, NY: Ballantine Books, 2000.

CHAPTER 8: GUIDED COMMUNICATION WITH LOT AND OTHER SPIRITS

Automatic Writing and Guided Communication

Mccoy, Edain. *How To Do Automatic Writing*. St. Paul, MN: Llewellyn Publications, 2002.

Mühl, Anita M. *Automatic Writing*. Whitefish, MT: Kessinger Publishing, LLC, 2003.

Strogen, Carol A. *When the Dead Speak to Us: The McWhorter Family Messages*, Kindle edition. Bloomington, IN: Xlibris Corporation, 2005.

Walsch, Neale Donald. *Conversations with God: An Uncommon Dialogue, Book 1*. New York, NY: G.P. Putnam's Sons, 1996.

---. *Conversations with God: An Uncommon Dialogue, Book 2*. Charlottesville, VA: Hampton Roads Publishing, 2014.

---. *Conversations with God. An Uncommon Dialogue, Book 3*. Charlottesville, VA: Hampton Roads Publishing, 2014.

CHAPTER 9: LIFE AND DEATH

Children's Books

Alexander, Pagyn. *Dreamtime Magic: Young Person's School of Magic & Mystery*. Jackson, TN: Dragonhawk Publishing, 2001.

Andrews, Ted. *Magic Of Believing: Young Person's School of Magic & Mystery*. Jackson, TN: Dragonhawk Publishing, 2000.

---. *Psychic Power: Young Person's School of Magic & Mystery*. Jackson, TN: Dragonhawk Publishing, 2000.

---. *Spirits, Ghosts & Guardians: Young Person's School of Magic & Mystery*. Jackson, TN: Dragonhawk Publishing, 2002.

---. *Faerie Charms: Young Person's School of Magic & Mystery*. Jackson, TN: Dragonhawk Publishing, 2003.

---. *Word Magic: Young Person's School of Magic & Mystery*. Jackson, TN: Dragonhawk Publishing, 2007.

---. *Healing Arts: Young Person's School of Magic & Mystery*. Jackson, TN: Dragonhawk Publishing, 2007.

---. *Divination & Scrying: Young Person's School of Magic & Mystery*. Jackson, TN: Dragonhawk Publishing, 2007.

Andrews, Ted, and Deborah Hayner. *Dreamsong of the Eagle*. Charlottesville, VA: Hampton Roads Publishing, 2003.

Bryant, Page. *Star Magic: Young Person's School of Magic & Mystery*. Jackson, TN: Dragonhawk Publishing, 2001.

Summer Rain, Mary. *Mountains, Meadows And Moonbeams: A Child's Spiritual Reader*. Norfolk, VA: Hampton Roads Publishing, 1992.

---. *Star Babies*. Charlottesville, VA: Hampton Roads Publishing, 1997.

Wesselman, Hank. *Little Ruth Reddingford and the Wolf: An Old Tale*. Bellevue, WA: Illumination Arts Publishing, 2004.

Past Life Regression

Andrews, Ted. *How to Uncover Your Past Lives*. St. Paul, MN: Llewellyn Publications, 2006.

Bowman, Carol. *Children's Past Lives: How Past Life Memories Affect Your Child*. New York, NY: Bantam Books, 1998.

---. *Return from Heaven: Beloved Relatives Reincarnated Within Your Family*. New York, NY: Harper Torch, 2003.

Modi, Shakuntala. *Remarkable Healings: A Psychiatrist Discovers Unsuspected Roots of Mental and Physical Illness*. Charlottesville, VA: Hampton Roads Publishing, 1998.

Stearn, Jess. *The Search for a Soul: Taylor Caldwell's Past Lives*. New York, NY: Berkley Books, 1994.

Virtue, Doreen. *Angel Medicine: How to Heal the Body and Mind with the Help of the Angels*. Carlsbad, CA: Hay House, 2004.

---. *Past-Life Regression with the Angels*. Audio CD. Carlsbad, CA: Hay House, 2006.

Spiritual Journeying

Altea, Rosemary. *Proud Spirit: Lessons, Insights & Healing from "The Voice of the Spirit World."* New York, NY: William Morrow Paperbacks, 1998.

---. *The Eagle and the Rose: A Remarkable True Story*. New York, NY: Grand Central Publishing, 2001.

Neff, Kelly Joyce. *Everyday Life in Two Worlds: A Psychic's Experience.* Charlottesville, VA: Hampton Roads Publishing, 1994.

CHAPTER 10: DAVID RETURNS

Courage: Live the Life You Desire
Kieves, Tama J. *This Time I Dance!: Creating the Work You Love.* New York, NY: TarcherPerigee, 2006.

Super Soul Sunday. OWNTV: Oprah Winfrey Network.

Health and Wellness
Hay, Louise L. *You Can Heal Your Life.* Carlsbad, CA: Hay House, 1987.

Hay, Louise L., Jim Brickman, and Michael A. Goorjian. *You Can Heal Your Life: The Movie.* Carlsbad, CA: Hay House, 2007.

LeClaire, Anne D. *Listening Below the Noise: A Meditation on the Practice of Silence.* New York, NY: Harper Perennial, 2010.

Sutherland, Caroline M. *The Body Knows: How to Tune In to Your Body and Improve Your Health.* Carlsbad, CA: Hay House, 2001.

---. *The Body Knows... How To Stay Young: Healthy-Aging Secrets from a Medical Intuitive.* Carlsbad, CA: Hay House, 2008.

Index

Chapter Resources

Book Club Questions
for Discussion

1. What do you believe happens when we die?

2. Have you ever had a spiritually transformative experience or a near death experience? Describe what happened. How did it make you feel? Did you share this with anyone?

3. Is there any part of *Change Maker* that seems unlikely to you? *Change Maker* describes true events as told from the author's perspective. What helps you believe this story is real or not real?

4. Are there components of *Change Maker* you would like to experience yourself? Where can you find the resources to assist your journey?

5. Do you feel the author's daily time spent in nature contributed to her spiritual development? Is there a natural location close to you that could assist your spiritual exploration?

6. Have you ever experienced an after-death communication or believe you received a sign from someone who has passed on? What happened and how did you feel?

7. Do you meditate? What type of meditative experience appeals to you? Is there a place in your home you can go to relax?

8. Do you enjoy any complementary health modalities such as Yoga, Reiki, Healing Touch, Tai Chi, Qigong or others? Have you ever requested any of these activities be provided to you when spending time in a hospital?

9. What do you think about angels or spirit guides? Do you believe everyone has spiritual beings that can assist us during our earthly existence or are guides only available to certain people?

10. Do you believe there are entities other than humans that interact with us on earth? Why or why not?

11. How does time impact your life? Have you ever tried to live without time? If so, when and how did you accomplish this? How does time make you feel? Does the concept of time continue for eternity?

12. What is love? Do you love yourself? Why or why not? Who do you love? How can you bring more love into your life?

Acknowledgements

This twenty-year book-writing project could have never been completed without fabulous assistance from dozens of people.

To my wonderful husband Jeff, thank you for your support the instant this incredible adventure started. Without your love, *Change Maker* would not be finished. Thank you from the center of my heart and soul. I look forward to spending eternity with you. Ken and Ryan, thank you for being the best sons a Mom could ever desire, and Jenny for being our magnificent new daughter-in-law. I am immensely proud of each one of you and all you are accomplishing. I love you very much. Dad and Mom, your understanding has been beyond belief. Thank you for being great role models, teaching me independence and giving me the courage to follow my dreams. My sisters Pam and Jiffy and your wonderful family members, thank you for being so loving and caring. Our bond is incredibly special. It's wonderful sharing my life with you.

To Micki McAllister, artist extraordinaire, thank you for the stunning illustrations that beautify *Change Maker*. I savored each moment we spent contemplating spirituality. Your heartfelt drawings capture nature's beauty and reflect each chapter's message perfectly.

Nancy Arael, thank you for teaching me the joys of living a spiritual life. The year we spent together was life changing. Your excellent training, guidance and love will remain with me forever.

Chris, Lori, Randy, Mohamed and your families, I love being cousins. I'm always excited to share family experiences especially during our annual summer gathering. Sue Apter, Toni Esposito, Heather Noll, Emma Mellon, Ingrid Jacobson, Ellen and Dan Erdman, Michelle Wasik, Colette Katz, Dottie Lutz, Becky Smith, Ned Ide, Kelly Shea, and Taylor Wallace, thank you for teaching me the meaning of friendship. To all the Clausen family members, thank you for your mahh-velous love and support for over 30 years. And to my new relatives, the Elphick, Smith and Porcino family and friends, it's GREAT joining our family with yours!

Grandma and Grandpa (Abe and Bessie) Dole and Granny and Gramps (Anne and William E.) Austill, thank you for surrounding me with love as I grew into adulthood. Uncle Allen and Aunt Joan Austill, it's fabulous sharing lives together, especially camping for close to 60 years of joy. I love you very much.

Lynn Lopez, you deserve special thanks for assisting me daily for over ten years. You are truly extraordinary. Bob Di-Sciullo, you are a gift. Thank you for giving me the freedom to publish *Change Maker*. Nancy Corson, your positive impact on the life of my family and myself has been profound. Carol Harding, thank you for letting me "practice" my skills with you. And all my work friends, thank you for being the best colleagues a gal could ever have. Each one of you is magnificent!

Judy Fort Brenneman, exemplary owner of Greenfire Creative, thank you for massaging my story into publish-ready status. I am eternally grateful for your excellent editorial and coaching skills. I would never have completed my book so successfully without your assistance. A million thanks forever.

To the fantastic team at She Writes Press, Publisher Brooke Warner, you exemplify the best in publishing support. Lauren Wise, your detailed Project Management assistance has been